Sunset
Barbecue
Cook Book

By the Editors of Sunset Books
and Sunset Magazine

Lane Publishing Co. • Menlo Park, California

EDITED BY Linda Brandt

SPECIAL CONSULTANTS: Joan Griffiths
Assistant Editor, Sunset Magazine

Will Kirkman

DESIGN: Helen Faibish

PHOTOGRAPHY: Norman A. Plate
with Lynne B. Morrall

ILLUSTRATIONS: Rik Olson

Editor, Sunset Books: David E. Clark

Fourth Printing May 1981

CONTENTS

EQUIPMENT & TECHNIQUES

The earliest barbecuers had little choice but to toss their meat into an open fire and cook it. Following generations refined this technique by devising handy tools and equipment—skewers, cooking grills, rotating spits, and detachable covers. Modern barbecuers no longer cook outdoors out of necessity, rather out of pleasure. Captivated by the aroma and tantalizing flavor of food cooked over an open fire, they continue to enjoy the oldest form of cooking, with the advantages of improved equipment and time-tested techniques.

Basic Types of Barbecues

Barbecues—charcoal-fired, gas, and electric—are manufactured in dozens of styles. The most common are the open brazier (either with or without a half-hood), the round covered kettle, and the rectangular covered barbecue with a hinged lid.

In addition to these three basic styles, there are several variations of the charcoal-fired barbecue. The hibachi (either single, double, or triple-brazier models) and the kamado (originally a Japanese smoke oven adapted for covered barbecue cooking) are two popular examples.

Open braziers

Back yard barbecue enthusiasts once did their cooking on large, permanently installed brick structures. Over the years, though, these have become less popular, thanks to the development of small, portable, metal fire boxes—the simplest and least expensive of which is the open brazier.

The open brazier lends itself to cooking pieces of food that lie flat and are no more than 2 inches thick, such as steaks, hamburgers, chops, fish, and chicken pieces. Since covered cooking on an open brazier is usually makeshift (an aluminum foil tent often serves as the cover), these braziers are less reliable for cooking roasts, whole birds, and thick pieces of meat. Roasts and birds can, however, be spit-roasted on the open brazier if you have the attachments.

Braziers come in a variety of sizes—from table-top portables to very large units that can cook enough food for a crowd. A good brazier should have a removable grill that is easy to adjust, and a bowl constructed of heavy metal that won't rust through at the bottom. You can protect the firebed bowl by lining it with sand and building your fire on the sand rather than directly on the metal bottom.

In addition, a good brazier should have three or four sturdy legs, with wheels on two of them. The legs should be firmly attached when in position, but should also be removable so you can conveniently transport your brazier to a picnic or campsite or store it when not in use.

Spit-roasting equipment, half-hoods, wind screens, and other attachments are available for some models, but not for all.

Covered kettle cookers

A covered kettle barbecue with adjustable dampers functions like a stove outdoors—it combines a broiler, smoker, oven, and grill. Heat is reflected off all surfaces (even the inside of the cover) back onto the food; and, since there are no open flames when the cover is on, flare-ups that could char food rarely occur.

Even the largest pieces of food can be cooked just the way you like, because you control the fire temperature by opening and closing dampers in the bottom and the cover. If the food is cooking too fast, lower the heat by closing the dampers a bit. To raise the heat, open the dampers to let in more air. And if there is still good charcoal left when you've finished cooking, close the dampers completely to snuff out the fire. You'll have leftover charcoal to relight next time.

Since kettles are designed for covered cooking, manufacturers recommend that you do *all* your barbecuing—from whole birds and roasts to hamburgers and chops—with the lid on. If you need to baste or turn the food, just hang the lid on the side rim of the barbecue.

Covered kettles come in many sizes, the average being about 40 inches high and 18 to 22 inches in grill diameter. When selecting which size to buy, consider the largest food you'll want to barbecue. If, for example, you're likely to do a medium to large turkey, make sure that the size you buy will accommodate it. Recently, barbecue manufactures have introduced kettles equipped with gas or electric grills. For more information, see "Gas and Electric Barbecues," page 8.

Barbecue boxes with hinged lids

Rectangular or box-shaped barbecues with hinged covers can be the most elaborate and expensive units. Some are portable, others are mounted on wagons, still others are permanently installed on pedestals. All work on the same principle as covered kettles—the cover turns the barbecue into an oven, and adjustable dampers allow you to control the fire temperature. You can adjust the distance between the food and coals by either raising or lowering the grill or fire grate; many models have a built-in air temperature thermometer that allows you to check the inside temperature when the lid is down.

A good barbecue box should be made of heavy metal with a resilient finish that won't be damaged by heat. Because of its construction, even the smallest barbecue box can be heavy and difficult to move about. Some models, though, are mounted on wagons instead of being attached to pedestals, so they can be moved, if necessary.

Cooking can be done with the lid open or closed, either directly on the grill or on some kind of spit-roasting attachment. Most manufacturers suggest closing the lid when a constant temperature is required for a specific length of time. Fast-cooking foods, such as hamburgers and hot dogs, can be grilled either with or without the lid.

Gas or electric grills, smoking equipment, rotisseries, spit baskets, special oven attachments, and convertible grills are available, depending on the model.

Hibachis & small portables

The pleasures of outdoor cooking need not be limited by the size of your yard—or even by lack of a yard. With a small, lightweight brazier or hibachi, you can barbecue anywhere—in the corner of a patio, at the beach, or on a picnic table.

Portability is the hibachi's greatest advantage. Most units disassemble easily or at least have legs that can be removed; some even fold in half, then slide into a carrying case. Because many small braziers are just scaled-down versions of standard barbecues, you often find similar accessory items: adjustable grills, special skewer holders, wind screens, even mini-rotisseries.

Since most units have about a 10 by 15-inch cooking surface, you are limited to cooking for a handful of people at one time. But you do save on fuel—just a few coals generate enough heat to cook the meal.

Tools & accessories

The world of barbecuing has produced its full share of gadgetry, both useful and frivolous. There are some necessary tools for cooking with and caring for the barbecue, as well as some extras you may or may not want.

Spit-roasting equipment. The basic accessory for any barbecue that will take it is spit-roasting equipment. At its simplest, this consists of spit support, an electric motor, and a pair of forks that slide onto the spit at each end to hold the food in place.

When buying this equipment, *be sure* it fits your particular model. Look for a sturdy spit that will not bend and a heavy-duty motor that will turn food evenly—even if it is slightly off balance. You can add weights, designed for balancing a spit, if the food is off balance; this makes it easier to rotate odd-shaped pieces such as whole birds or rib roasts. It is also helpful to have extra forks for cooking more than one piece of food at a time, and pliers for tightening and releasing fork screws.

Basic tools. These are the tools you'll need for everyday use of the barbecue: *long tongs* for adjusting hot coals and turning food; a *stiff metal brush* for scrubbing the grill; *mitts* for emergency adjustment of the grill or spit; *long-handled forks* and *spatulas;* and a dozen or so *long-handled skewers*.

Other tools that can be useful include a hinged grill with long handles for holding and turning hot dogs or fish, packages of aluminum pans in various sizes to use as drip pans under large roasts and spit-roasted food, a meat thermometer, and charcoal rails for stacking coals.

Additional attachments. An enormous number of attachments, accessories, and gadgets are manufactured for barbecues. While all may be handy for a particular type of cooking, think of these items as extras: special Dutch ovens, smoking equipment, automatic skewer turners, griddles, special racks for holding odd-shaped roasts, detachable utensil holders, all-weather barbecue covers, and a cylindrical basket that fits your spit and tumbles pieces of food such as chicken or ribs.

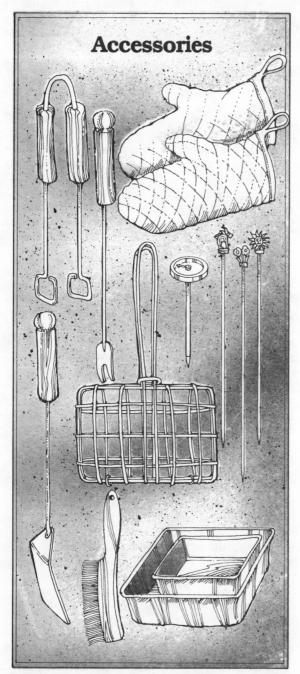

Accessories

USEFUL BARBECUE ACCESSORIES include (top) long-handled tongs and fork, thick mittens; (center) spatula, hinged wire broiler, meat thermometer, metal skewers; (bottom) metal brush and aluminum drip pans.

Basic Barbecue Styles

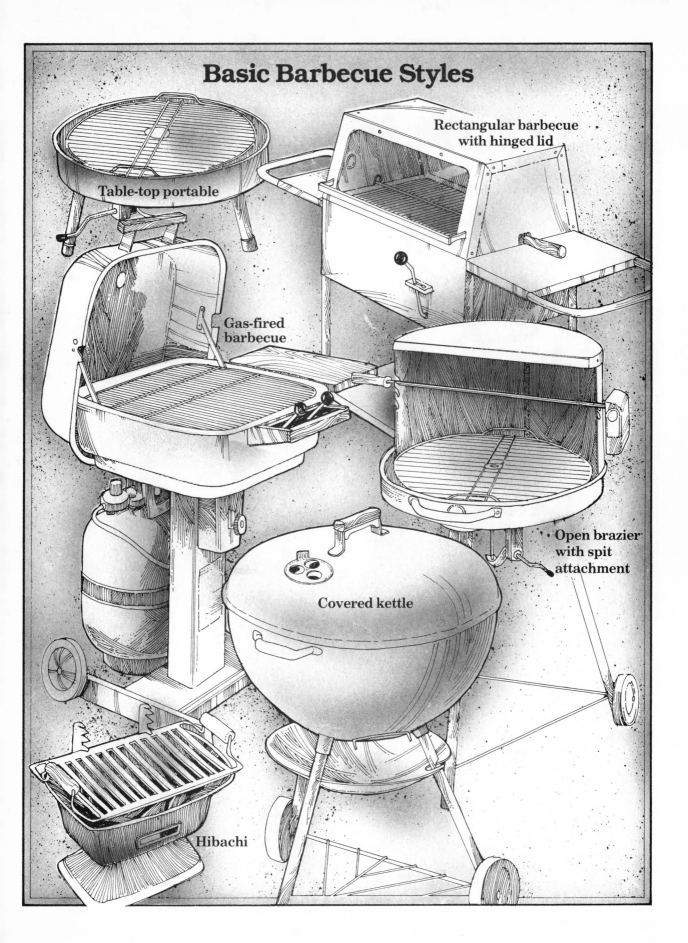

Table-top portable

Rectangular barbecue
with hinged lid

Gas-fired
barbecue

Open brazier
with spit
attachment

Covered kettle

Hibachi

Gas & Electric Barbecues

Two alternatives to charcoal-fired barbecues are those that use either gas or electricity. There are kettles and single or double box-shaped units that use natural or bottled gas. Barbecues heated by electric coils are available in a similar array of styles. Both the gas and electric models save you the trouble of building the fire as well as cleaning up the ashes. Since most units require only a brief preheating, there's little waiting for the grill once the food is ready to cook.

Outdoor units that use bottled gas usually roll on wheels; natural gas units are mounted on a fixed pedestal and need to be connected to a permanent gas line. Electric units are more portable, since they merely plug into the nearest outlet.

Indoors, permanently installed gas and electric units are often located near range tops so that they can share the existing overhead exhaust fan. Some barbecues have their own, though.

Gas units and some electric ones employ a special briquet-shaped material, such as lava rock, above the burner to radiate heat evenly. When meat juices drip on the hot lava rock briquets, smoke rises and penetrates the meat. It's the smoke—not the use of charcoal—that gives food an authentic "barbecue" flavor.

As a rule, food prepared on gas and electric grills requires about the same amount of cooking time as on conventional barbecues. If you have a gas or electric unit, check the manufacturer's instructions for cooking information for your particular model.

Methods of Cooking

Each type of barbecue lends itself to different kinds of cooking. In our recipes, you will see the words *Open grill, Covered grill, Spit-roasted,* or *Skewer-cooked* directly below the recipe name, to indicate the recommended method of cooking.

Some recipes, such as those for whole birds and large roasts, may suggest covered grill *or* spit-roasted. This indicates that these recipes can be done either in a covered barbecue or on a spit. You'll also notice that some open grill recipes include a second cooking time—for covered grill cooking. Most open grill recipes easily convert to covered grill ones without any difference in cook-

ing time; but for those that don't, the additional information is provided.

Cooking on a grill
Steaks, chops, roasts, meat patties, sausages, whole fish, poultry, skewered foods—virtually anything can be cooked on a barbecue grill. The size and type of food determine whether you need to use an open or closed grill. Here is the difference between the two.

Open grill. With this method, food is cooked on a metal grill without the use of a hood or attached cover. Built-in brick barbecues, braziers, hibachis and other small portables, and some rectangular boxes are designed for this method of cooking. (Kettles can be used for open grill cooking, too, in spite of the fact that manufacturers usually suggest keeping the cover on most of the time.)

Pieces of food that lie fairly flat and are no more than about 2 inches thick are good candidates for open grill cooking directly over a solid bed of coals (see illustration, page 11). When barbecuing thicker pieces on an open grill, use a simple tent of aluminum foil to trap some heat.

We recommend setting the grill about 6 inches above the heat source, but an adjustable grill is very helpful. The adjustment may be a screw-type central shaft that you regulate by spinning the grill or cranking the handle, or it may be as simple as a grill support with several different positions.

Open grill cooking over solid bed of coals

Covered grill. All kettles and rectangular units come with a lid that may be closed for cooking. They are ideal for cooking on windy or cold days.

Dampers on the lid and under the firebox allow you to adjust the flow of air and thus control the heat. It's the heat, reflected from all sides and from the top, that provides for even cooking and gives the effect of an oven.

Covered grill cooking is necessary for whole birds and large or very thick pieces of meat that call for slow, even cooking. For foods like these, you cook over a divided bed of coals, with the coals banked on each side of a drip pan or around it (see illustration, page 11).

Covered grill cooking over divided bed of coals

Spit-roasting

When you roast meat or poultry on a spit, the juices and bastes roll around the surface of the meat rather than drip off into a pan or into the fire. The meat cooks slowly over the coals (see illustration, page 11) and bastes itself, thus staying moist and flavorful.

To spit-roast on a brazier, you will need a half-hood attachment to hold the spit and motor in place. If you want to adjust the spit, move it up or down in the series of slots in the hood. To spit-roast on a covered rectangular barbecue, you'll need to buy the accessories sold for that unit. Instead of adjusting the spit, you adjust the firebed by moving a suspended tray of burning coals up or down while the spit stays fixed.

Though spit-roasting equipment is sold for some kettle barbecues, many users feel that it is unnecessary, since kettles do a good job of browning upper surfaces of roasts and large birds.

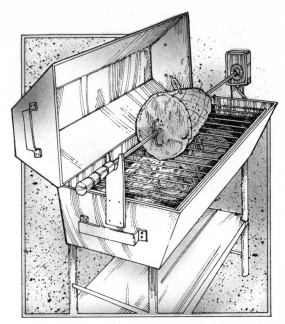

Spit-roasting with motorized attachment

Skewer-cooking

The most versatile barbecue method is probably skewer-cooking, because it can be adapted to any size and type barbecue. Everything from pieces of meat, fish, or poultry to vegetables and fruits can be skewered in various combinations and then roasted right on the grill, with or without a cover. As the kebabs cook, you can baste them with butter, oil, or a marinade, or you can create self-basting ones by threading a partially cooked bacon slice over and under each food chunk.

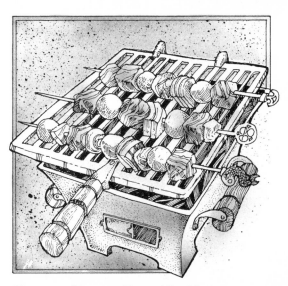

Skewer-cooking on table-top hibachi

When preparing different foods ahead of time, keep in mind their cooking requirements. Those that just need heating—fruits and canned or pre-cooked foods—can be skewered in larger portions than those that require cooking. Group together the longer-cooking foods, such as meats; later you can add to the grill the skewers of foods that cook quickly. On a tiny hibachi with just a few coals, food should be in fairly small pieces. On larger grills with hotter fires, you can use larger pieces—up to 1½ to 2 inches on a side—and push them more tightly together. Packed skewers will cook more slowly, and center chunks will be pinker.

Charcoal Fires

We have tried to standardize instructions for fuel use and fire building, but as any outdoor cook knows, there are variables that affect each type of barbecue. The arrangement of coals and the number you need depend basically on two things—the size of your firebed and the type of food you're cooking.

When we refer to charcoal, we mean briquets—the pressed, pillowlike squares of charcoal that are widely available. If you compare various kinds, you'll discover that they vary somewhat in density and composition. Some burn longer than others—often up to twice as long (the package may specify "long-burning"). Fast-burning brands force you to use more charcoal during cooking to maintain heat. Therefore, we based our testing on long-burning briquets, and our instructions and descriptions of fire types reflect this.

Charcoal should not be burned indoors without proper ventilation, as the carbon monoxide it produces can be fatal.

How many briquets? When preparing a solid bed of coals in an average brazier or kettle (18 to 22 inches in diameter), you will need 25 to 35 long-burning briquets to cook your food. About 30 to 40 briquets are needed for a divided bed and for a spit-roasting fire.

Another way to calculate the number of coals is to lay enough briquets to form a solid bed that is slightly bigger than the grill area needed for whatever you're cooking. A third way is to imagine your firebed as a grid made up of 6-inch squares. Each square should hold nine briquets, so multiply nine by the number of squares that suits the size of your food.

When barbecuing large pieces of meat or foods that take more than 40 to 50 minutes to cook, you will need to add more charcoal. A good rule is to add 5 or 6 briquets every ½ hour to maintain a constant temperature. Place the briquets directly on hot coals, spacing them evenly over the existing fire area. With a divided bed of coals, add 5 or 6 briquets to each side.

Reusing briquets. Often coals are left over after food is cooked. By all means extinguish them and use them again later. If you have a brazier or hibachi, the best way to smother the hot coals is to remove them from the barbecue with long tongs and place them in a tightly covered metal container, such as a small garbage can. If you have a covered barbecue, simply close all the dampers after cooking to extinguish coals. Since the coals are already partially consumed, you will have to judge their value as fuel by their appearance rather than by actually counting pieces.

Starting the Fire

Old hands have their favorite ways to start a barbecue. Some use a fire chimney; others use starter fluids or solid starter blocks right in the firebed; still others like an electric starter.

Fire chimney. If you don't want to buy one, improvise—fire chimneys are simple to make. Remove the top and bottom of a 2-pound coffee can and punch holes just above the bottom edge with nails or a traditional can opener that makes triangular holes. Stack briquets inside, on top of two wadded sheets of newspaper or a few pre-treated briquets (see below); then light. You'll have burning coals ready to use in about 30 minutes. Remove the chimney and spread the coals.

Liquid starter. If you use a liquid starter, be sure it's a product intended for charcoal. Some volatile substances, like gasoline, are very dangerous and may explode. *Don't pour any liquid starter on hot coals, even if they seem to have gone out,* because the coals could suddenly flare up.

If you're using either a chimney or a flammable starter, you can *pretreat briquets* for a quicker start. Soak a few briquets in a jar filled with liquid starter. When it's time to light the fire, place the pretreated briquets on the bottom of the firebed or chimney can and add the remaining briquets.

Solid starter. A relatively new type of barbecue starter, designed to provide fast, sure ignition of charcoal without sparks and without chemical residue or aftertaste, is known as solid starter. Sold under various brand names, these small (about 1 by 2 inches), compressed, woodlike blocks or sticks light easily with the touch of a match and continue to burn with no attention until coals are ready for cooking in 30 to 40 minutes.

Electric starter. Set an electric starter in the firebed on a few coals. Pile the remaining coals on top, then plug in the starter. After about 10 minutes, unplug it and remove it from the coals. (If you leave the starter plugged in any longer, the heating element may burn up.)

The Shape of Your Fire

The shape of your fire is determined by what you plan to barbecue. Quickly cooked foods are grilled over the direct heat of a solid bed of coals, while fatty foods or those requiring a long, slow roasting time are cooked over the indirect heat of a divided bed of coals. Spit-roasted food requires a special arrangement of coals.

Solid bed of coals. The shape of fire producing the most intense, direct heat consists of a solid bed of coals spread uniformly under the food and extending an inch or two beyond it on all sides. If the fire gets too hot, spread out the coals to provide a cooling air space between them. If the coals cool down, increase the heat by pushing them together and knocking off white ash residue, or by adding more briquets, or both.

Solid bed of coals

Divided bed of coals. A pile of coals banked on each side of a metal drip pan is used to produce indirect heat. In some barbecues, coals may completely surround the drip pan. Food is placed on the grill above the pan rather than over the coals, thereby preventing any chance of flareup.

Divided bed of coals

Spit-roasting bed of coals. Coals are arranged in one solid rectangular bed about 6 inches across and extending 3 or 4 inches beyond each end of the spitted food. Imagine a wall extending from spit to firebed; then arrange the band of coals about 2 inches behind this imaginary wall. Place a metal drip pan directly beneath and in front of the food. Every ½ hour add 5 or 6 briquets, spacing them evenly, to maintain a constant temperature.

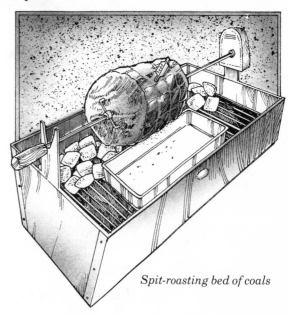

Spit-roasting bed of coals

When to Start Cooking

We use three different terms in our recipes to describe fire temperature at the start of cooking. The hottest—called "glowing"—is the first usable state the fire reaches. The less-hot states are reached as the fire burns down and begins to cool.

Glowing describes the hottest fire, one in which coals are just reaching the gray ash stage. If you hold your hand near the grill over this fire, 2 or 3 seconds is all you can tolerate. A fire of this sort is good for searing meat.

Medium-glowing describes coals as they begin to cool down and are partially covered with gray ash. You could not hold your hand near the grill over this fire for more than 3 or 4 seconds. A medium-glowing fire is necessary for quick-cooking foods that have a tendency to scorch (such as those with sugar in the baste).

Low-glowing describes coals that are completely covered with a thick, gray ash. If you hold your hand near the grill over this fire, you should be able to keep it there for 4 or 5 seconds before the heat forces you to remove it. Low-glowing fires are used primarily for cooking thick pieces of meat for a long period.

BEEF

No other meat is barbecued as much as beef, partly because
it's so delicious — the subtle flavor readily picking up
a smoky tinge — and partly because it makes experts out of
newcomers to the art of outdoor cookery. Like no other
method of cooking, a charcoal fire has a way of searing in
the fine juices of a steak on the grill or a roast
turning on its spit. Burgers, steaks, chops, and
flat roasts need to be cooked on the grill; round
or thick-cut roasts, though, benefit from spit-roasting
or from being cooked under cover.

Basic Recipe: Hamburgers

Open or covered grill • Cooking time: 6-12 minutes

What compares with a grilled hamburger served on a toasted bun with catsup and perhaps a slice of onion or tomato? You can glorify a basic burger in any number of different ways.

Try crusty French rolls or English muffins instead of buns. Another possibility is toasted rye bread — it's especially good with cheeseburgers. Offer a selection of relishes and cheese slices, or provide different sauces such as homemade mayonnaise, Thousand Island or green goddess dressing, or even blue cheese dressing for the adventuresome.

Do you want a quick and simple supper? Try chile burgers: hamburgers on toasted buns with a spoonful of thick chile ladled over each. Or you might experiment with slices of jack cheese and chopped green chiles — they can transform ordinary patties into south-of-the-border delights.

Good hamburgers depend on the grade of ground beef you use. At your meat counter, you may find three or more different grades of ground beef, each containing a different amount of fat — usually between 15 and 30 percent. Experience will tell you which you prefer. Our recipes simply call for lean ground beef.

3 pounds lean ground beef
 Salt and pepper
8 hamburger buns, split and buttered

Shape meat into 8 patties. Since the loss of fat during cooking causes meat to shrink a bit, patties should be made a little larger than the buns.

Place patties on lightly greased grill 4 to 6 inches above a solid bed of glowing coals. Cook, turning once, for 3 to 4 minutes on each side for rare or until done to your liking when slashed. Season with salt and pepper. Place buns, cut-side-down, around edges of grill to heat. Serves 8.

Basic Recipe: Grilled Steak

Open or covered grill • Cooking time: 10-30 minutes

Most outdoor cooks say "steak" when they think of barbecuing beef. Porterhouse, sirloin tip, top round, T-bone or New York—whichever you select, it's best if the meat is 1 to 2 inches thick.

Turn meat only once while it's cooking and salt it *after,* rather than during, cooking. Remember not to puncture the steak when you turn it — this causes flavorful juices to sizzle out onto the fire. Flip it over gently with tongs or a spatula.

1 beef steak (about 3 lbs.), cut 2 inches thick or
 6 to 8 individual steaks (10 to 14 oz. *each*),
 cut 1 to 2 inches thick
 Baste (optional)
 Salt and pepper
 Flavored butter (optional)

Slash any fat around edge of steak about every 4 inches. This keeps the steak from curling during cooking. (Be sure to slash fat just *to* the meat, not into it.) Place steak on lightly greased grill 4 to 6 inches above a solid bed of glowing coals. For large steak, cook, turning once and basting occasionally (if desired), for 12 to 15 minutes per side for rare. For covered grill cooking, reduce total cooking time by 5 minutes. For individual steaks, cook 5 to 8 minutes on each side for rare or until done to your liking when slashed.

Transfer steak to a serving platter; season with salt and pepper. Slash top in a crisscross pattern 5 or 6 times and, if desired, spread with about 2 tablespoons of flavored butter (see Flavored Butters for Beef, page 14). Carve large steak into thin slanting slices to serve. Makes 6 to 8 servings.

Basic Recipe: Beef Roast on a Covered Grill

Covered grill • Cooking time: About 1½ hours

Any 3 to 5-pound boneless beef roast will cook in less than 2 hours on a covered grill. Our recipe calls for a cross-rib roast but other cuts like sirloin tip work equally well. For less tender cuts of beef like a rump roast, it's best to use a marinade (see Favorite Beef Marinades & Bastes, page 14).

Beef roast marinade (recipe follows)
3 to 5-pound boneless cross-rib roast, tied

Prepare beef roast marinade. Place roast in a deep, close fitting bowl, or in a plastic bag in a rimmed dish; pour marinade over roast. Cover bowl or twist and tie bag closed; refrigerate until next day.

Bank about 20 medium-glowing coals on each side of fire grill and place a metal drip pan in center. Place grill 4 to 6 inches above drip pan; grease grill lightly.

Lift meat from marinade and drain briefly (reserve marinade). Insert a meat thermometer into center of thickest portion. Place meat on grill directly over drip pan. Cover barbecue and adjust dampers according to manufacturer's directions. Cook, basting occasionally with reserved marinade, for about 1½ hours for rare or until meat thermometer registers 135°. Add 5 or 6 briquets to each side of fire every ½ hour to maintain a constant temperature. When roast is cooked, let it stand for about 20 minutes, then slice thinly and serve with meat juices. Makes 10 to 12 servings.

Beef roast marinade. Blend together ⅓ cup **catsup**, ¾ cup **dry red wine**, ½ cup **salad oil**, 1 tablespoon *each* **instant minced onion** and **Worcestershire**, 1 teaspoon dry **rosemary**, 1½ teaspoons **salt**, ¼ teaspoon **pepper,** and about 5 drops **liquid smoke seasoning** (optional).

Favorite Beef Marinades & Bastes

No clear distinction exists between a baste and a marinade, but a sauce used during cooking is usually called a baste, and one used to tenderize or flavor the meat before cooking is called marinade.

A simple baste need only be a little butter or oil brushed over the meat to seal it and keep the juices from running out. The addition of an acid, such as wine, vinegar, or lemon juice, makes the sauce a marinade because it helps to tenderize the meat. Herbs, spices, and other ingredients may also be added for flavoring.

Allow meat to marinade for at least one hour and be sure to turn it several times so flavors can penetrate thoroughly. The following marinades are sufficient to tenderize most cuts of meat, but for less tender cuts, you might first want to apply unseasoned meat tenderizer.

Herb-Wine Marinade Baste
Blend ⅓ cup tomato-based **chili sauce** or catsup, ¾ cup **dry red wine**, ½ cup **salad oil**, 1 tablespoon *each* **instant minced onion** and **Worcestershire**, 1 teaspoon crumbled dry **rosemary**, 1½ teaspoons **salt**, ¼ teaspoon **pepper**, and ¼ teaspoon **liquid smoke** (optional).

Teriyaki Marinade
Combine 2 tablespoons **salad oil**, ⅓ cup **soy sauce**, 2 tablespoons firmly packed **brown sugar**, 1 tablespoon Japanese **sake** or dry sherry, 1 teaspoon grated fresh **ginger** or ¼ teaspoon ground ginger, and 1 clove **garlic** (minced or pressed).

Wine Garlic Marinade
Combine 1 cup **dry red wine**, 2 tablespoons **wine vinegar**, 2 cloves **garlic** (minced or pressed), 1 teaspoon **oregano leaves**, and 2 tablespoons **salad oil**.

Flavored Butters for Beef

You can use flavored butters to season barbecued beef either during the grilling or right before serving. Most are not intended for long-time storage; for best flavor, plan to use them within a week or two.

Shallot Butter
In a wide frying pan over medium heat, melt 2 tablespoons **butter**. Add 1 medium-size **onion** (finely chopped) and cook until soft. Add 2 tablespoons **dry sherry** and cook until liquid evaporates. Cool thoroughly, then combine with ½ cup (¼ lb.) **butter** or margarine (at room temperature) and ¼ teaspoon **salt.** Beat until fluffy; cover and refrigerate until ready to use.

Fines Herbes Butter
Combine ½ cup (¼ lb.) **butter** or margarine (at room temperature), 1 tablespoon *each* minced **parsley** and chopped **chives,** ½ teaspoon *each* **tarragon leaves** and **dry chervil**, ¼ teaspoon **salt,** and dash of **pepper.** Beat until fluffy. Cover and refrigerate until ready to use.

Garlic Butter
Combine ½ cup (¼ lb.) **butter** or margarine (at room temperature), 2 or 3 cloves **garlic** (minced or pressed), and 2 tablespoons minced **parsley.** Beat until fluffy. Cover and refrigerate until ready to use.

Red Onion Butter
In a wide frying pan over medium heat, melt 2 tablespoons **butter**. Add 1 medium-size **red onion** (finely chopped) and cook until soft. Add 2 tablespoons **dry red wine** and cook until liquid has evaporated. Cool thoroughly, then combine with ½ cup (¼ lb.) **butter** or margarine (at room temperature) and ¼ teaspoon **salt.** Whirl in blender or beat until fluffy. Cover and refrigerate until ready to use.

Cheeseburgers with Guacamole

Open or covered grill • Cooking time: About 10 minutes

With these burgers you mix the cheese right in with the meat. For a Mexican flavor, top them off with a dollop of guacamole.

1½ pounds lean ground beef
½ teaspoon *each* garlic salt and onion salt
1 teaspoon Worcestershire
1½ cups shredded Cheddar cheese
1 large avocado, peeled, pitted and mashed
1 tablespoon lemon juice
3 drops liquid hot pepper seasoning

Blend beef, garlic salt, onion salt, Worcestershire, and cheese. Shape into 4 patties, each about 1 inch thick. To make guacamole, blend avocado with lemon juice and hot pepper seasoning; set aside.

Place patties on lightly greased grill 4 to 6 inches above a solid bed of glowing coals. Cook, turning once, for 3 to 4 minutes on each side for rare. Serve with a dollop of guacamole on top. Makes 4 servings.

Stretched Hamburgers

Open or covered grill • Cooking time: About 15 minutes

Just a pound of lean ground beef makes eight nutritious burgers when blended with a mixture of finely chopped vegetables. Serve on toasted buns with sliced tomatoes and cucumbers.

- 1 pound lean ground beef
- 2 carrots, shredded
- 2 stalks celery, finely chopped
- 1 sprig parsley, finely chopped
- 1 small green pepper, seeded and finely chopped
- 1 medium-size onion, finely chopped
- 1 clove garlic, minced or pressed
- 1 tablespoon meat seasoning sauce
- 1 egg
- 2 tablespoons salad oil
  Salt and pepper
- 8 hamburger buns, split and buttered
- 8 large tomato slices
  Cucumber slices

Blend beef, carrots, celery, parsley, green pepper, onion, garlic, seasoning sauce, egg, salt, pepper, and oil. Shape into 8 patties.

Place on lightly greased grill 4 to 6 inches above a solid bed of glowing coals. Cook, turning once, for 6 to 7 minutes on each side or until done to your liking when slashed. When you turn patties, place buns, cut-side-down, around outside of grill to toast. Season with salt and pepper; serve on buns with tomato and cucumber slices. Serves 8.

Crunchy Onion Burgers

Open or covered grill • Cooking time: About 10 minutes

Just before cooking, add crisp, canned French-fried onions for a surprising flavor and texture.

- 1½ pounds lean ground beef
- 1 teaspoons salt
- ⅛ teaspoon pepper
- 1 tablespoon catsup
- 1 can (3½ oz.) French-fried onions, crumbled
- 6 hamburger buns or English muffins, split and buttered

Mix together beef, salt, pepper, catsup, and onions. Shape into 6 patties, each about 1 inch thick.

Place patties on lightly greased grill 4 to 6 inches above a solid bed of glowing coals. Cook, turning once, for 3 to 4 minutes on each side for rare. When you turn patties, place buns, cut-side-down, around outside of grill to toast. Makes 6 servings.

Soy-dipped Hamburgers

Open or covered grill • Cooking time: About 10 minutes

Prepared at home, these hamburger patties can be marinating while you are en route to a picnic site. After you grill them, serve with thinly sliced tomatoes and green pepper rings.

- ½ cup *each* soy sauce and water
- 1 clove garlic, minced or pressed
- 2 teaspoons grated fresh ginger root
- 2 tablespoons Worcestershire
- 6 tablespoons firmly packed brown sugar
- 3 pounds lean ground beef
- 8 hamburger buns or French rolls, split and buttered
  Thinly sliced tomatoes
  Green pepper rings

Combine soy, water, garlic, ginger, Worcestershire, and sugar. Shape meat into 8 patties, each about 1 inch thick, and place in a plastic bag. Pour in marinade, twist and tie bag closed. Refrigerate or place in picnic cooler and marinate for 1 to 2 hours.

Lift patties from marinade and drain briefly (reserve marinade). Place patties on lightly greased grill 4 to 6 inches above a solid bed of glowing coals. Cook, turning once and basting with reserved marinade, 3 to 4 minutes on each side for rare. When you turn patties, place buns, cut-side-down, around outside of grill to toast. Serve on toasted buns with thinly sliced tomato and green pepper rings. Makes 8 servings.

Giant Burger for Eight

Open or covered grill • Cooking time: About 12 minutes

A whole loaf of round French bread or peda bread is the foundation for a huge meat patty. We used a large, hinged wire broiler to grill the meat, but you can also cook directly on a grill. To turn the giant patty, you need two rimless baking sheets. Slip one sheet under the meat; place the other sheet on top. Invert the patty and slide it back onto the grill. *(Pictured on page 18)*

   ½ cup (¼ lb.) butter or margarine, at room
      temperature
   ½ teaspoon *each* prepared mustard and
      chili powder
   1 round loaf French bread or peda bread
   3 pounds lean ground beef
   2 teaspoons seasoned salt
   ½ cup finely chopped green onion
      (including some tops)
   2 tablespoons tomato-based chili sauce
   1 tablespoon soy sauce *or* Worcestershire
   1 large red onion, thinly sliced
      Shredded lettuce
   2 large tomatoes, thinly sliced
   1 large avocado, thinly sliced

Blend together butter, mustard, and chili powder. Split bread horizontally. (If you are using French bread, cut it horizontally into thirds and reserve center slice for another use.) Spread the two pieces of bread with butter mixture. Combine meat with seasoned salt, green onion, chili sauce, and soy. Shape into one large patty, slightly bigger than the bread.

Place patty on lightly greased grill 4 to 6 inches above a solid bed of glowing coals. Cook, turning once (see instructions above), for 5 to 6 minutes per side for rare or when done to your liking when slashed. When you turn patty, place bread, cut-side-down, on outside of grill to toast.

To assemble, place meat patty on bottom half of toasted bread, top with onion slices, shredded lettuce, tomato and avocado slices, and top of bread. Cut in pie-shaped wedges to serve. Makes about 8 servings.

Ground Beef Cordon Bleu

Open or covered grill • Cooking time: About 10 minutes

Here's an excellent choice for the first night in camp, and it's a gourmet treat besides. Herb-flavored melted cheese is hidden inside each patty.

   1 pound lean ground beef
   2 slices Swiss cheese
      Garlic salt
      Dry basil
   4 hamburger buns, split and buttered
      Sour cream

Divide meat into 8 equal portions and shape into very thin patties — about ¼ inch thick. On 4 patties, place a half slice of Swiss cheese, folding in corners so there is a border of meat all around. Sprinkle with a little garlic salt and a pinch of basil, then place a second patty on top and press edges to seal.

Place patties on lightly greased grill 4 to 6 inches above a solid bed of glowing coals. Cook, turning once, for 3 to 4 minutes on each side for rare. When you turn patties, place buns, cut-side-down, around outside of grill to toast. Serve with a dollop of sour cream on top. Makes 4 servings.

Lebanese Hamburgers

Open or covered grill • Cooking time: About 40 minutes

A typical Lebanese spice mixture of cinnamon, paprika, and cayenne flavors not only the hamburgers but the accompanying onions as well. Since the onions require long, slow cooking, they can be done ahead and reheated later.

   3 teaspoons *each* ground cinnamon,
      paprika, and salt
   ¾ teaspoon cayenne
   ½ cup (¼ lb.) butter or margarine
   4 large onions, peeled, halved lengthwise,
      and sliced
   4 small tomatoes
   3 pounds lean ground beef (or ½ beef and
      ½ lamb)
   ½ cup water
  12 hamburger buns, split and buttered
      Yogurt sauce (recipe follows)

Combine cinnamon, paprika, salt, and cayenne; set aside. In a wide frying pan, melt 6 tablespoons of the butter over low heat; add onion and cook, stirring often, until onion is very tender and beginning to brown (about 40 minutes). When onion has cooked for about 20 minutes, add 4 teaspoons of the spice mixture. When onion is done, transfer to a heat-proof dish and place in a 300° oven to keep warm, or refrigerate for later use.

Cut tomatoes into ½-inch-thick slices. In a wide frying pan over medium heat, melt the remaining 2 tablespoons butter; add tomatoes and cook, turning once, for 1 to 2 minutes on each side. Remove onions from oven and arrange tomatoes over them; pour in any juice from tomatoes and return dish to oven.

In a bowl, blend remaining spice mixture with meat and water. Shape into 12 patties, each about 4 inches in diameter. Place patties on well greased grill 4 to 6 inches above a solid bed of glowing coals. Cook, turning once, for 6 to 8 minutes on each side for medium rare. When you turn patties, arrange buns, cut-side-down, around outside of grill to toast. Serve patties on buns and offer tomato-onion mixture and yogurt sauce as accompaniments. Makes 12 sandwiches.

Yogurt sauce. Combine 2 cups **unflavored yogurt,** 1 teaspoon **salt,** 1 clove **garlic** (minced or pressed), and 1 tablespoon finely chopped fresh **mint.**

Steak & Cheese Sandwiches

Open or covered grill • Cooking time: About 15 minutes

Slices of flank steak are mounded on toasted English muffins, then topped with Münster cheese and minced green onion.

> ⅓ **cup dry red wine**
> 3 **tablespoons salad oil**
> ¼ **teaspoon** *each* **thyme and marjoram leaves**
> 1 **clove garlic, minced or pressed**
> ¼ **cup chopped onion**
> 1 **flank steak (about 1½ lbs.)**
> 6 **English muffins, split and buttered**
> ½ **pound Münster cheese, sliced**
> **Minced green onion**

Combine wine, oil, thyme, marjoram, garlic, and onion. Pour over steak, cover, and refrigerate for 4 hours or until next day.

Lift steak from marinade and drain briefly. Place on lightly greased grill 4 to 6 inches above a solid bed of glowing coals. Cook, turning once, for 5 to 7 minutes on each side for medium rare or until done to your liking when slashed. When you turn steak, place muffins, cut-side-down, around outside of grill to toast.

To serve, cut meat across the grain in thin, slanting slices. Place alternating slices of meat and cheese on 6 muffin halves. Sprinkle with onion and top with remaining muffin halves. Makes 6 servings.

Steak Sandwich with Mushroom Sauce

Open or covered grill • Cooking time: About 15 minutes

Leftover marinade becomes part of the sauce for these steak-on-rye sandwiches.

> ½ **cup dry red wine**
> ½ **medium-size onion, cut in chunks**
> 2 **tablespoons lemon juice**
> ¼ **cup olive oil or salad oil**
> 1 **clove garlic**
> ½ **teaspoon salt**
> ⅛ **teaspoon pepper**
> 1½ **pounds top sirloin steak, about 1 inch thick**
> **About 6 tablespoons butter or margarine**
> 1 **pound medium-size mushrooms, sliced**
> 6 **slices light rye bread, buttered**
> **Chopped parsley for garnish**

In a blender combine wine, onion, lemon juice, oil, garlic, salt, and pepper. Whirl until blended. Pour over steak, cover, and refrigerate 1 to 2 hours.

Remove steak from marinade and drain briefly (reserve marinade); set steak aside. In a wide frying pan, melt 4 tablespoons of the butter over medium heat. Add mushrooms and cook for about 5 minutes. Add reserved marinade and turn the heat to high. Boil mixture, stirring constantly, until just slightly reduced and thickened. Keep warm while steak cooks.

Place steak on lightly greased grill 4 to 6 inches above a solid bed of glowing coals. Cook, turning once, for about 8 minutes on each side for rare or until done to your liking when slashed.

When you turn steak, place bread, butter-side-down, around outside of grill to toast. To serve, cut meat across the grain in thin, slanting slices. Place a few slices on each piece of toast, cover with mushroom sauce and sprinkle with parsley. Makes 6 servings.

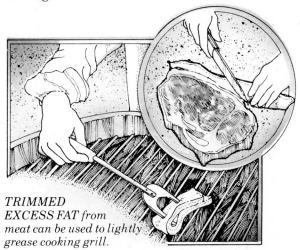

TRIMMED EXCESS FAT from meat can be used to lightly grease cooking grill.

Teriyaki Flank Steak

Open or covered grill • Cooking time: About 12 minutes

Typical seasonings for Japanese teriyaki give a special flavor to this flank steak. The marinade can be stored in the refrigerator and used again with another piece of meat.

  ½ **cup soy sauce**
  1 **clove garlic, minced or pressed**
  1 **teaspoon ground ginger**
  2 **tablespoons** *each* **firmly packed brown**
      sugar, lemon juice, and salad oil
  1 **tablespoon instant minced onion**
  ¼ **teaspoon pepper**
  1 **flank steak (about 1½ lbs.)**

Combine soy, garlic, ginger, brown sugar, lemon juice, oil, onion, and pepper. Pour over steak, cover, and refrigerate for 6 hours or until next day.

Lift steak from marinade and drain briefly (reserve marinade). Place on lightly greased grill 4 to 6 inches above a solid bed of glowing coals. Cook, turning once and basting with reserved marinade, for about 6 minutes on each side or until done to your liking when slashed.

To serve, cut meat across the grain in thin, slanting slices. Makes 4 servings.

Mexican Flank Steak Sandwiches

Open or covered grill • Cooking time: About 15 minutes

Spoon zesty avocado-tomato dressing over cheese-covered slices of barbecued beef piled high on a toasted French roll. If you prefer, substitute warmed flour tortillas for rolls.

  ½ **cup olive oil or salad oil**
  ¼ **cup** *each* **red wine vinegar, lime juice,**
      and finely chopped onion
  1 **teaspoon** *each* **sugar and oregano leaves**
  2 **cloves garlic, minced or pressed**
  ½ **teaspoon salt**
  ¼ **teaspoon ground cumin**
  1 **flank steak (about 1½ lbs.)**
  6 **French or steak rolls, split**
    Bottled jalapeña sauce
    About 12 ounces sliced jack cheese
    Avocado-tomato dressing (recipe
      follows)

SANDWICHED IN ROUND LOAF of peda bread, an oversize meat patty with lettuce, onion and tomato slices, and wedges of avocado becomes a giant burger for eight. (Recipe on page 16)

Combine oil, vinegar, lime juice, onion, sugar, oregano, garlic, salt, and cumin. Pour over steak, cover and refrigerate for 6 hours or overnight; turn occasionally.

Lift steak from marinade and drain briefly. Place on lightly greased grill 4 to 6 inches above a solid bed of glowing coals. Cook, turning once, for 5 to 7 minutes on each side for medium rare or until done to your liking when slashed. When you turn steak, place rolls, cut-side-down, around outside of grill to toast.

To serve, cut meat across the grain in thin, slanting slices. Divide slices among toasted rolls and top each with a small amount of jalapeña sauce, sliced cheese, and several spoonfuls of avocado-tomato dressing. Makes 6 servings.

Avocado-tomato dressing. Peel, pit, and mash 2 ripe **avocados,** add 1 tablespoon **lemon juice,** and ½ teaspoon **salt** (or substitute two 8-ounce packages frozen avocado dip, thawed). Add a few drops **liquid hot pepper seasoning, 2 tomatoes** (peeled and diced), ½ cup chopped **onion,** and ½ cup chopped fresh **coriander** (cilantro) or 1 tablespoon dry cilantro leaves or ¼ cup chopped parsley.

Steak & Blue Cheese Butter

Open or covered grill • Cooking time: About 10 minutes

Flank steak first marinates in French dressing, then is served with a blue cheese and chive-flavored butter. If you wish, prepare the butter ahead and refrigerate, but warm to room temperature before serving.

    Bottled French-style salad dressing
  1 **flank steak (about 1½ lbs.)**
  ¼ **cup butter or margarine, at room**
      temperature
  ½ **cup blue-veined cheese, crumbled**
  1 **clove garlic, minced or pressed**
  1 **tablespoon chopped chives**
  2 **tablespoons brandy**

Pour salad dressing over steak, cover, and refrigerate for 4 hours or until next day. Blend butter, cheese, garlic, chives, and brandy together; refrigerate, if made ahead.

Lift steak from marinade and drain briefly. Place on lightly greased grill 4 to 6 inches above a solid bed of glowing coals. Cook, turning once, for about 5 minutes on each side for rare. Transfer steak to a warm platter. To serve, cut meat across the grain in thin, slanting slices. Spoon blue cheese butter over each serving. Makes about 4 servings.

Hickory-smoked Meats

The tantalizing flavor and rich mahogany color of smoke-cooked meats tempt many an outdoor cook to try smoke-cooking.

Our versatile technique—smoking first with hickory chips in a covered barbecue, then oven-roasting—is equally successful for beef, pork, turkey, and chicken. The trick is to maintain a consistently low temperature in your barbecue by using just a few hot coals at a time, and using an oven thermometer to check the temperature frequently. Hot coals and presoaked hickory chips are then added at regular intervals throughout the 4 to 5-hour smoking period to maintain the low temperature.

Plan to do the smoking at least a day before you serve the meat. If you want cold meat for slicing, smoke and roast it well ahead. If you want to serve it hot, do the smoking any-time ahead, then finish roasting just before serving.

Basic Instructions

You'll need a covered barbecue with a tight-fitting lid or dome high enough to enclose the meat you plan to smoke. Have ready 16 to 20 whole long-burning briquets, 1 to 1½ pounds hickory or other hardwood chips, a small barbecue or old shallow metal pan for holding extra hot coals, an accurate oven or meat thermometer, and long-handled tongs for lifting hot coals.

On the fire grill or lower rack of the bar-becue, mound and ignite 12 briquets. When briquets are completely covered with gray ash, push 4 coals to each side of fire grill, as far over as possible.

Place remaining 4 hot coals in separate barbecue or pan; add several unignited coals so you will have a continuous supply of extra hot coals. (Every time you add a hot coals to your barbecue during smoking, add an unig-nited one to small barbecue to keep up your supply.)

Place 3 to 4 cups hickory chips in a bowl of water to soak for 20 minutes. (Every time you add hickory chips to the fire, add more hickory chips to water as needed to keep up the supply.)

Between the hot coals, center a foil drip pan. Grease cooking grill lightly and rotate it so you have access to heating coals. Place meat on grill (be sure no part of meat extends over coals); place thermometer beside or on top of meat near center of grill.

Scoop out 2 handfuls of soaked chips; let drain briefly, then sprinkle 1 handful over each group of burning coals on each side of drip pan. (Use a long skewer to spread evenly.) Cover barbecue and adjust dampers to the open position.

Check thermometer after 10 minutes. If temperature is below 140°, add a hot coal to one side. Above 150°, remove a coal until proper temperature is attained. Continue to check every 30 or 40 minutes. When smoke is no longer coming out of vents, add another handful of soaked drained chips to each group of coals. Also check thermometer; add or sub-tract coals as needed to maintain 140° to 150°. (You'll need to add about 1 coal each hour.)

Meats and poultry will be smoked enough when they're golden brown (usually between 3 and 4½ hours). Lift meat off grill to a roast-ing pan. Remove drip pan; save drippings for gravy, if desired.

To serve meat hot, let it cool to room tem-perature, wrap in foil, and refrigerate up to 3 days; freeze for longer storage. On the day you plan to serve the meat (defrost if frozen), finish roasting it in the oven. To serve meat cold, oven-roast it right after smoking, then refrigerate until ready to use.

Beef roast
Purchase a 3 to 5-pound rolled and tied bone-less beef roast such as sirloin tip or cross rib. Smoke-cook as directed in Basic Instructions for 3 hours or until golden brown. To complete cooking, insert a meat thermometer into thickest part and roast in a 325° oven for 45 minutes (about 60 minutes if refrigerated) or until meat thermometer registers 140° for rare. Let stand for 15 minutes, then carve and serve hot. Or, cool, cover and refrigerate; cut in thin slices and serve cold.

Beef brisket
Purchase a 4 to 6-pound fresh or corned beef brisket. Place in a large kettle with enough

water to cover and simmer for 2½ hours or until tender; drain (reserve cooking water). Smoke-cook as directed in Basic Instructions for 2 hours or until fat is golden brown. Return brisket to cooking water; bring to boiling, remove from heat, let stand for 15 minutes, then carve, and serve hot. Or cool completely in water, drain, cover, and refrigerate; cut in thin slices and serve cold.

Pork roast
Purchase a 3 to 6-pound rolled and tied bone-in or boneless pork loin roast. Smoke-cook as directed in Basic Instructions for 3 hours or until golden brown. To complete cooking, insert a meat thermometer into thickest part and roast in a 325° oven for about 1 to 1½ hours (1½ to 2 hours, if refrigerated) or until thermometer registers 170°. Let stand for 15 minutes, then carve and serve hot. Or cool, cover, and refrigerate; slice and serve cold.

Whole turkey
Purchase a 15 to 20-pound turkey; defrost, if frozen. Remove neck and giblets and reserve for other uses. Rinse turkey inside and out; pat dry. Fasten neck skin to back with skewers. Tie wings to body or tuck them in back of bird, akimbo-style. Leave legs untied. Smoke-cook as directed in Basic Instructions for 4 to 4½ hours or until golden brown.

If turkey is to be served hot, you may want to stuff it; do this after bird has been smoked and just before basting. Lightly fill neck cavity with stuffing; again fasten neck skin to back with skewers. Then lightly stuff body cavity; tuck a piece of foil over cavity opening. (Don't stuff turkey if you plan to serve it cold.)

Place bird, breast-side-up, on rack in shallow roasting pan. Insert meat thermometer into thickest portion of thigh (make sure it doesn't touch bone). Brush with melted butter or margarine and loosely cover with foil. Roast in a 325° oven, basting occasionally with butter, for 2 to 2½ hours (3½ to 4 hours, if refrigerated) or until meat thermometer registers 180° to 185°. Let stand for 20 to 30 minutes before carving; serve hot. Or cool, wrap in foil, and refrigerate to serve cold.

Turkey breast
Purchase an 8 to 9-pound whole turkey breast (or a 4 to 5-pound breast half). Remove bones, if desired, for easier slicing. Smoke-cook as directed in Basic Instructions for 2½ to 3 hours or until skin is golden brown. To complete cooking, insert a meat thermometer into thickest part and roast in a 325° oven for about 40 minutes (about 60 minutes, if refrigerated) or until thermometer registers 170°. Let stand for 15 minutes, carve and serve hot. Or cool, cover, and refrigerate; cut in thin slices and serve cold.

Whole chicken
Purchase a 3 to 5-pound whole broiler-fryer or roasting chicken. Tie wings to body or tuck them in back of bird, akimbo-style; leave legs untied. Smoke-cook as directed in Basic Instructions for 2 to 2½ hours or until golden brown. To complete cooking, roast in a 325° oven for about 30 minutes (about 60 minutes, if refrigerated) or until leg jiggles and juices run clear. Let stand for 15 minutes, then carve and serve hot. Or cool, cover, and refrigerate; cut in pieces and serve cold.

Flank Steak & Orange Slices

Open or covered grill • Cooking time: About 15 minutes

A popular Brazilian combination is barbecued beef marinated in orange juice and accompanied by slices of fresh oranges. *(Pictured on opposite page)*

    1 flank steak (about 1½ lbs.)
    ½ cup orange juice
    2 tablespoons instant minced onion
    2 cloves garlic, minced or pressed
    ¼ teaspoon pepper
    3 tablespoons salad oil
    2 tablespoons red wine vinegar
    ¾ teaspoon ground cumin
    2 or 3 large oranges, peeled and sliced

Trim any excess fat from steak. Combine orange juice, onion, garlic, pepper, oil, vinegar, and cumin. Pour over steak, cover, and refrigerate, turning steak occasionally, until next day.

Lift steak from marinade and drain briefly (reserve marinade). Place on lightly greased grill 4 to 6 inches above a solid bed of glowing coals. Cook, turning once and basting several times with reserved marinade, for 5 to 7 minutes on each side for medium rare or until done to your liking when slashed.

To serve, cut meat across the grain in thin, slanting slices. Garnish with orange slices. Makes 4 servings.

Chef's Chuck Roast

Open or covered grill • Cooking time: About 1 hour

Choose a chuck roast cut extra thick so that when you grill it over a hot fire, the finished roast is dark and crusty on the outside but still very pink in the center.

    2 cloves garlic, minced or pressed
    2 tablespoons olive oil or salad oil
    ¼ teaspoon dry mustard
    1 teaspoon soy sauce
    ¼ teaspoon *each* dry rosemary and
        Worcestershire
    2 tablespoons wine vinegar
    ¼ cup dry white wine
  1½ teaspoons meat seasoning sauce
    1 chuck roast (about 5 lbs.), cut 2½ inches
        thick

Cook garlic in oil over low heat, just until it softens (do not brown). Add mustard, soy, and rosemary. Remove from heat and stir in vinegar, wine, Worcestershire, and seasoning sauce. Pour over meat,

cover, and refrigerate until next day, turning occasionally.

Lift meat from marinade and drain briefly (reserve marinade). Brush roast with some of the marinade before placing on a lightly greased grill 4 to 6 inches above a solid bed of glowing coals. Cook, turning once and basting occasionally with reserved marinade, for about 55 minutes or until well browned on both sides and done to your liking when slashed. For covered grills, reduce cooking time by about 10 minutes.

To serve, cut meat across the grain in thin, slanting slices. Makes about 6 servings.

Savory Chuck Roast

Open or covered grill • Cooking time: About 1½ hours

This simple-to-make chuck roast has a full-flavored spicy barbecue sauce to accompany it.

    1 medium-size onion, thinly sliced
    4 tablespoons olive oil or salad oil
    1 clove garlic, minced or pressed
    ½ cup thinly sliced celery
    ¾ cup *each* tomato-based chili sauce and
        catsup
    ½ cup water
    2 tablespoons *each* Worcestershire, wine
        vinegar, and lemon juice
    1 teaspoon *each* prepared horseradish and
        prepared mustard
    1 teaspoon hickory smoked salt
      Few drops liquid hot pepper seasoning
    ½ teaspoon pepper
    3 tablespoons firmly packed brown sugar
    ½ cup dry sherry
    1 chuck roast (about 5 lbs.), cut 2 inches
        thick
      Unseasoned meat tenderizer

Separate onion into rings. Heat oil in a wide frying pan over medium heat; add onion and cook until limp. Add garlic, celery, chili sauce, catsup, water, Worcestershire, vinegar, lemon juice, horseradish, mustard, smoked salt, hot pepper seasoning, pepper, and sugar. Bring to a boil, then simmer, uncovered, for 20 minutes. Add sherry and simmer for 10 minutes more.

Apply tenderizer to meat according to package directions. Brush meat on both sides with sauce and place on lightly greased grill 4 to 6 inches

(Continued on page 24)

GARNISHED WITH ORANGE SLICES,
flank steak marinates overnight in
orange juice before searing over hottest
coals on the barbecue. (Recipe above left)

above a solid bed of glowing coals. Cook, turning once and basting occasionally with sauce, for 40 to 50 minutes for rare or until done to your liking when slashed. For covered grill, reduce cooking time by 10 minutes. Makes 4 to 6 servings.

Beef Teriyaki

Open grill • Cooking time: About 5 minutes

You can quickly cook thin strips of teriyaki beef if you lay them flat on a hibachi grill; or you can skewer them first and then grill them.

> 1 flank steak (about 1½ lbs.)
> 1 cup regular-strength beef consommé (or use ½ cup dry red wine)
> ⅓ cup soy sauce
> ¼ cup chopped green onion (including some tops)
> 1 clove garlic, minced or pressed
> 3 tablespoons lime juice
> 2 tablespoons firmly packed brown sugar or honey

Partially freeze meat; then cut it across the grain in thin, slanting slices, about ¼ inch thick. Combine consommé, soy, onion, garlic, lime juice, and brown sugar. Pour over meat, cover, and refrigerate until next day.

Lift meat from marinade and drain briefly (reserve marinade). Place on a lightly greased, very hot grill about 4 inches above a solid bed of glowing coals. Cook, turning once and basting with reserved marinade, for about 1 or 2 minutes on each side. Makes 5 to 6 servings.

Chuck Steak with Lemon-Anchovy Butter

Open or covered grill • Cooking time: 30–40 minutes

At serving time, each guest tops his or her serving of barbecued steak with a slice of lemon-anchovy butter cut from a butter ring garnish.

> ½ cup (¼ lb.) butter or margarine, at room temperature
> 1 teaspoon lemon juice
> 1 can (2 oz.) anchovy fillets, drained
> Chopped parsley
> Unseasoned meat tenderizer
> 1 chuck steak (3½ to 4 lbs.), cut 1½ inches thick

Combine butter, lemon juice, and anchovies; mash thoroughly with a fork until smooth. Blend in about 1 teaspoon parsley; shape into a ring, ball, or loaf, place on a bed of parsley and chill.

Apply tenderizer to meat according to package directions. Place on lightly greased grill 4 to 6 inches above a solid bed of glowing coals. Cook, turning once, for about 30 to 40 minutes or until well browned and done to your liking when slashed. For covered grills, reduce cooking time by 10 minutes. Serve with the butter ring garnish so guests can top their steak with slices of the lemon-anchovy butter. Makes 4 to 6 servings.

Sirloin Steak Skewers

Skewer cooked • Cooking time: 15–18 minutes

You marinate cubes of steak in a wine-herb marinade, then grill them for a simple and delicious main dish.

> ¾ cup dry red wine
> 3 tablespoons *each* olive oil (or salad oil) and lemon juice
> 2 cloves garlic, minced or pressed
> ¼ teaspoon *each* dry rosemary and thyme leaves
> 3 pounds top sirloin steak, cut into 1½-inch cubes

Combine wine, oil, lemon juice, garlic, rosemary, and thyme. Pour over meat, cover, and refrigerate for 4 hours or until next day.

Lift meat from marinade and drain briefly. Divide meat equally among 6 to 8 sturdy metal skewers and place on lightly greased grill 4 to 6 inches above a solid bed of glowing coals. Cook, turning often, for 15 to 18 minutes or until well browned on all sides and done to your liking when slashed. Makes 6 to 8 servings.

Barbecued Prime Rib Bones

Open or covered grill • Cooking time: 20–25 minutes

If you relish the sweet meat that clings to bones, you'll find that two or three meaty standing ribs can make a delicious meal. These are the bones that are trimmed away when the butcher makes a boned and rolled rib roast, so the meat is tender and can be quickly grilled until richly browned outside and juicy pink within. Allow about 1 pound per person.

> About 6 pounds standing rib bones
> Mustard or tangy tomato marinade (recipes follow)

Arrange bones in a large shallow pan. Prepare one of the marinades and pour over ribs; turn bones to coat all sides. Cover and set aside at room temperature for about 2 hours.

Lift bones from marinade and drain briefly (reserve marinade). Place on lightly greased grill 4 to 6 inches above a solid bed of glowing coals. Cook, turning and basting frequently with reserved marinade, for 20 to 25 minutes for medium rare or until done to your liking (cut a gash to test). Makes about 6 servings.

Mustard marinade. In a small bowl, combine ⅓ cup **Dijon mustard** and 2 tablespoons **red wine vinegar.** While beating constantly with a wire whip, add ¼ cup **olive oil** or salad oil a few drops at a time. Then add 1 clove **garlic** (minced or pressed), ½ teaspoon *each* **thyme leaves** and **Worcestershire,** and ¼ teaspoon **pepper.** Stir together until well combined.

Tangy tomato marinade. In a pan, stir together 1 can (8 oz.) **tomato sauce,** 1 tablespoon **Dijon mustard,** ¼ cup red wine **vinegar,** 1 tablespoon packed **brown sugar,** 1 clove **garlic** (minced or pressed), 1 teaspoon **oregano leaves,** ½ teaspoon **Worcestershire,** and ¼ teaspoon **pepper.** Bring to a boil, reduce heat, and simmer, uncovered, for 5 minutes to blend flavors; stir several times. Cool to room temperature before pouring over meat.

Santa Fe Shortribs

Covered grill • Cooking time: 40–50 minutes

Flavored with mild chile *salsa,* these lean and meaty beef ribs cook to perfection in a covered barbecue.

> Unseasoned meat tenderizer
> 6 pounds lean shortribs, cracked
> 1½ cups dry red wine
> 3 tablespoons olive oil or salad oil
> 1 small onion, chopped
> 2 cloves garlic, minced or pressed
> 1 teaspoon salt
> ½ teaspoon pepper
> 1 bay leaf
> ½ cup bottled red chile salsa

Apply tenderizer to meat according to package directions. Combine wine, oil, onion, garlic, salt, pepper, bay leaf, and chile salsa. Pour over meat, cover, and refrigerate for 4 hours or until next day.

Lift ribs from marinade and drain briefly (reserve marinade). Place on lightly greased grill 4 to 6 inches above a solid bed of glowing coals. Cover barbecue and adjust dampers according to manufacturer's directions. Cook, turning and basting occasionally with reserved marinade, for 40 to 50 minutes or until well browned on all sides and

done to your liking when slashed. Makes about 8 servings.

Western Barbecue Steak

Open or covered grill • Cooking time: About 25 minutes

This ever-popular, spicy barbecue sauce is excellent on any cut of beef. You can use a large steak or several smaller ones in this recipe.

> 2 or 3 tablespoons bacon drippings, butter, or margarine
> ½ cup finely chopped onion
> ⅓ cup lemon juice
> 2 tablespoons catsup
> 1 tablespoon *each* Worcestershire and prepared horseradish
> 1 teaspoon paprika
> ⅛ teaspoon pepper
> 1 large clove garlic, minced or pressed
> 2 bay leaves
> About 4 pounds steak, at least 1 inch thick

Melt bacon drippings in a saucepan over medium heat; add onion and cook until limp. Remove from heat and stir in lemon juice, catsup, Worcestershire, horseradish, paprika, pepper, garlic, and bay leaves. Pour over steak and marinate for 30 minutes at room temperature, turning once.

Lift steak from marinade and drain briefly (reserve marinade). Place steak on lightly greased grill 4 to 6 inches above a solid bed of glowing coals. Cook, turning once and basting occasionally with reserved marinade, for about 12 minutes on each side for a single 2-inch-thick steak, or about 8 minutes on each side for several 1-inch-thick steaks. Makes 6 to 8 servings.

FLAVORFUL JUICES STAY PUT when you turn barbecued meat with tongs rather than piercing with fork.

Pepper Steak

Open or covered grill • Cooking time: About 10 minutes

Hot, herb-scented tomato slices adorn this classic pepper steak. Warm brandy is ignited, then spooned over meat just before serving.

    1 teaspoon coarsely crushed black pepper
    4 small New York steaks or club steaks, cut
        1 inch thick
    3 tablespoons butter or margarine
    2 large firm tomatoes
    ⅛ teaspoon *each* dry basil and garlic salt
    4 tablespoons brandy

Sprinkle pepper over both sides of steaks; press and force it into surfaces. Allow steaks to stand for 30 minutes.

Melt butter over medium heat in a wide frying pan. Slice tomatoes about ½ inch thick and cook until just heated through. Transfer to a platter. Season with basil and garlic salt; keep warm.

Place steaks on lightly greased grill 4 to 6 inches above a solid bed of glowing coals. Cook, turning once, for about 5 minutes on each side for rare or until done to your liking when slashed. Arrange steaks on warm platter with tomato slices. Warm and ignite brandy before spooning over steak. Makes 4 servings.

Whole Fillet & Blue Cheese

Open or covered grill • Cooking time: About 30 minutes

A whole fillet of beef—the filet mignon—is cooked quickly and served with a tangy blue cheese butter.

    1 cup (½ lb.) butter or margarine, at room
        temperature
    ¼ pound blue-veined cheese
    1 tablespoon chopped chives or chopped
        green onion
        Finely chopped parsley
    1 fillet of beef (4 to 6 lbs.)
        Salad oil
        Watercress

Blend butter, cheese, and chives together until smooth. Shape into a log, roll in parsley, wrap in wax paper, and refrigerate until firm.

Place fillet on lightly greased grill 4 to 6 inches above a solid bed of glowing coals. Cook, turning and brushing with oil to brown, for about 30 min-

GARDEN FRESH VEGETABLES
with hot, buttery garlic sauce for bagna
cauda, pop-open clams, skewers of
teriyaki sliced pork and jumbo prawns
make tempting hot hors d'oeuvres served
right from grill. (Pages 28, 29, and 85)

utes for rare or until done to your liking when slashed.

Unwrap butter and place on a bed of watercress. Cut meat in thick slices; pass butter as condiment for meat. Makes 8 to 10 servings.

Steak with Rosemary

Open or covered grill • Cooking time: About 30 minutes

Flavored only with fresh rosemary, a thick porterhouse or sirloin steak grilled on a barbecue is both simple and special. *(Pictured on page 31)*

    2 tablespoons fresh rosemary or 2
        teaspoons dry rosemary
    1 porterhouse or sirloin steak (about 4 lbs.),
        cut 2 inches thick
        Salt and pepper

Press rosemary firmly into both sides of meat. Place steak on lightly greased grill 4 to 6 inches above a solid bed of medium-glowing coals. Cover and adjust dampers according to manufacturer's directions.

Cook, turning once, for about 15 minutes on each side for rare. Sprinkle with salt and pepper and cut meat across the grain in thin, slanting slices. Makes 6 to 8 servings.

Sirloin Steak Mirabeau

Open or covered grill • Cooking time: About 15 minutes

Anchovy fillets and pimento-stuffed olives create a decorative garnish for the top of this barbecued steak. Carve it in thin, slanting slices to serve.

    1 tablespoon butter or margarine, at room
        temperature
    1 teaspoon anchovy paste
    1 sirloin steak (about 2½ lbs.), cut 1 inch
        thick
        Freshly ground pepper
    1 can (2 oz.) anchovy fillets, drained
    ½ cup pimento-stuffed olives, halved

Combine butter and anchovy paste; set aside. Place steak on lightly greased grill 4 to 6 inches above a solid bed of glowing coals. Cook, turning once, for 6 to 8 minutes on each side for rare or until done to your liking when slashed.

Transfer steak to serving platter, sprinkle with ground pepper, and arrange anchovies in a crisscross pattern over top. Arrange olive halves in each open square. To serve, cut meat across the grain in thin, slanting slices. Makes 4 to 6 servings.

Hors d'oeuvres

Why not simplify outdoor entertaining by relying on a barbecue to help you out? Let your guests cook their own hors d'oeuvres, serving themselves right from the grill.

Grilled Sausages & Cheese

Open or covered grill • Cooking time: About 20 minutes

Small, hearty sandwiches, made by topping French rolls with hot cheese and a piece of sausage, are sure to please any appetite.

> About 1 pound mild Italian-style pork sausage
> About 1½ pounds teleme or mild jack cheese
> About ¼ pound mozzarella cheese, shredded
> 1 loaf (1 lb.) slender-shaped French bread, sliced; *or* about 6 French rolls, sliced

Place sausage in large pan, cover with water, and bring to boiling. Then reduce heat and simmer, covered, for 15 minutes. Drain and set aside.

Cut teleme cheese into thick slices and spread over a 10 by 14-inch rimmed metal platter or pan (you can also use a shallow wok). Sprinkle mozzarella over teleme.

Place precooked sausage on lightly greased grill 4 to 6 inches above a small solid bed of medium-glowing coals (coal bed should be equal to the area of the cheese pan). Cook, turning frequently, for about 6 minutes or until well browned on all sides; push to a cool area of barbecue. Set cheese platter on grill directly over heat, place bread in a cooler area, and cover barbecue with hood or drape loosely with foil. When cheese is melted (about 5 to 8 minutes) push pan away from direct heat; slice sausage and place at one end of pan.

Let guests serve themselves, making small sandwiches of French bread with a spoonful of cheese and a slice of sausage. Makes 8 to 10 servings.

Chinese Pork Appetizers

Skewer-cooked • Cooking time: 7–10 minutes

Cinnamon, cloves, and anise flavor the pork for these unusual hot appetizers. Thread them on individual metal skewers for easier handling. *(Pictured on page 26)*

> ¼ cup soy sauce
> 2 tablespoons salad oil
> 2 cloves garlic, minced or pressed
> 1 small, dried, hot chile pepper, crushed
> ½ teaspoon sugar
> ¼ teaspoon anise seed
> ⅛ teaspoon *each* ground cinnamon and cloves
> 2 pounds lean pork, cut into 1-inch wide strips

Combine soy, oil, garlic, pepper, sugar, anise, cinnamon, and cloves in a bowl. Add pork strips and stir gently to coat each piece. Cover and refrigerate for 1 to 2 hours.

Thread 1 or 2 strips of meat onto individual skewers. Place on lightly greased grill 4 to 6

inches above a solid bed of medium-glowing coals. Cook, turning occasionally, for 7 to 10 minutes or until done to your liking. Makes about 2 dozen appetizers.

Pop-open Clams

Open grill • Cooking time: 6–7 minutes

Here's a popular recipe that allows each guest to prepare his own hot appetizer. Place clams, paper napkins, and a small fork for each person next to the barbecue. Allow 6 to 8 clams per serving. *(Pictured on page 26)*

36 to 48 clams, well scrubbed in fresh water
6 tablespoons melted butter or margarine

Arrange cleaned clams in a large bowl near barbecue. Pour melted butter into a heat-resistant pot and place on cooler section of grill to keep warm.

Place clams directly on grill 4 to 6 inches above a solid bed of low-glowing coals. After about 3 minutes or when clams begin to open, turn them over and continue to cook until they pop wide open. Have guests, protecting their fingers with napkins, hold clams over butter pot to drain clam juices into butter. They then pluck out clams with their forks, dip in butter, and eat. Makes about 6 servings.

Bagna Cauda

Open grill • Cooking time: About 5 minutes

Here's a colorful, serve-yourself appetizer of fresh raw vegetables that are dipped in a hot, buttery garlic and anchovy sauce. *(Pictured on page 26)*

How to Serve
Because you want to keep that fresh-from-the-garden look, cut vegetables just enough to make it easy for guests to break away portions to eat. Arrange vegetables in a basket of appropriate size. Provide a dish or small bowl in which guests can place discarded pieces of vegetables. Alongside the basket of vegetables, place the hot butter-oil sauce (recipe follows). Also present a basket of thinly sliced

French bread or sliced crusty rolls.

To eat, swirl a piece of vegetable through the hot sauce. Hold a piece of bread like a napkin under the vegetable as you lift it. The bread will catch any drips and become very tasty itself.

Bagna Cauda Vegetables
You'll need about 1 or 2 cups vegetable pieces per person, but estimate quantities while vegetables are still whole. Choose a colorful assortment. If you wash and prepare vegetables early in the day, store them in plastic bags or cover with clear plastic wrap and refrigerate for as long as 6 to 8 hours. Sprinkle with water just before serving.

Artichokes. Offer whole cooked artichokes. To eat, bite off tender base of each bract.

Carrots. Leave on an inch of stem; peel. Gash carrot not quite through in short crosswise sections; break apart to eat.

Cauliflower. Cut out core, keeping head whole. Break off flowerets to eat.

Cherry tomatoes. Dip with stems to eat.

Green peppers. Cut vertically down to the stem in 8 to 12 sections around seed center. Break to eat.

Mushrooms. Trim stem ends. Eat small mushrooms whole. Cut large ones through cap only into 4 or 6 sections; break to eat.

Radishes. Cut off root ends and all but 1 or 2 leaves to hold for dipping.

Zucchini and yellow crookneck squash. Trim ends; cut not quite through in short sections. Break apart to eat.

Hot Butter-Oil Sauce
Choose a heat-resistant container that will hold twice the amount of sauce you make. In it, combine ½ cup (¼ lb.) butter, ¼ cup olive oil, and 4 small cloves garlic (minced or pressed). Thoroughly drain 1 can (2 oz.) flat anchovy fillets, finely chop and add to sauce.

Place container on grill 4 to 6 inches above a small, solid bed of medium-glowing coals. Heat until mixture bubbles. Move to a cooler section of the grill *(mixture must not get hot enough to brown and burn)*. Makes 8 to 10 servings.

Swiss Mustard Steak

Open or covered grill • Cooking time: About 30 minutes

When this steak is almost ready, you assemble mustard sauce in a rimmed serving platter. As you slice the meat, its juices blend into the sauce. Swirl each piece in the sauce as you serve.

  1 boneless top sirloin steak or top round
     steak (sometimes called London broil),
     cut 2 to 3 inches thick
  1 clove garlic
  ¼ cup dry vermouth or dry white wine
  1 tablespoon Dijon mustard
  ¼ teaspoon Worcestershire
  ⅛ teaspoon *each* crushed dry rosemary and
     basil, oregano leaves, and tarragon
     leaves
     Salt and pepper

Place steak on lightly greased grill 4 to 6 inches above a solid bed of glowing coals. Cook, turning once, for about 15 minutes on each side for rare or until done to your liking when slashed.

To serve, crush garlic in bottom of a warm rimmed steak platter. Stir in wine, mustard, and Worcestershire. Sprinkle rosemary, basil, oregano, and tarragon over top and stir again. Place steak on platter, setting it in sauce. Salt and pepper to taste. Cut meat across the grain in thin, slanting slices. Swirl each piece in sauce before transferring to individual plates. Makes 8 to 10 servings.

Crusty Barbecued Cross Rib Roast

Covered grill • Cooking time: 1¾–2 hours

A cross rib roast is a boned and rolled chuck roast, and you get the same delicious flavor when you barbecue.

  ¼ cup *each* salad oil and apple juice
  ½ cup strong black coffee
  1 tablespoon fennel seed
  ½ teaspoon onion powder
  ⅛ teaspoon pepper
  1 cross rib roast (5 to 6 lbs.), about 6 inches
     in diameter
     Salt

Combine oil, apple juice, coffee, fennel, onion powder, and pepper. Pour over meat, cover, and let stand for 1 to 2 hours, turning often.

Bank about 20 medium-glowing coals on each side of fire grill and place a metal drip pan in center. Place grill 4 to 6 inches above drip pan; grease grill lightly.

Lift meat from marinade and drain briefly (reserve marinade). Insert meat thermometer into thickest portion of center of roast. Place meat on grill directly over drip pan. Cover barbecue and adjust dampers according to manufacturer's directions. Cook, basting occasionally with reserved marinade, for 1¾ to 2 hours or until meat thermometer registers 135° for rare. Add 5 or 6 briquets on each side of fire every ½ hour to maintain a constant temperature. Makes 10 to 12 servings.

Sesame Beef Roast

Covered grill • Cooking time: 1½–1¾ hours

This delicious, sesame-flavored roast beef benefits from marinating for a full day. Select a cross rib or sirloin tip roast weighing about 4 pounds.

  ⅓ cup sesame seed
  ½ cup *each* salad oil and soy sauce
  ⅓ cup lemon juice
  2 tablespoons white wine vinegar
  1 tablespoon sugar
  2 cloves garlic, minced or pressed
  1 medium-size onion, sliced
  1 boneless cross rib or sirloin tip roast
     (about 4 lbs.)

Heat a small dry pan over medium heat; add sesame seed and cook until golden brown, then remove from heat. Add oil, soy, lemon juice, vinegar, sugar, garlic, and onion. Pour over meat, cover, and refrigerate until next day, turning occasionally.

Bank about 20 medium-glowing coals on each side of fire grill and place a metal drip pan in center. Place grill 4 to 6 inches above drip pan; grease grill lightly.

Lift meat from marinade and drain briefly (reserve marinade). Insert meat thermometer into thickest portion of center of roast. Place meat on grill directly over drip pan. Cover barbecue and adjust dampers according to manufacturer's directions. Cook, basting occasionally with reserved marinade, for 1½ to 1¾ hours or until meat thermometer registers 135° for rare. Add 5 or 6 briquets on each side of fire every ½ hour to maintain a constant temperature. Makes 6 to 8 servings.

FLAVORED WITH FRESH ROSEMARY,
thick-cut broiled steak (recipe on page 27) complements bacon and cheese-stuffed potatoes in foil (recipe on page 88) and vegetable kebabs (recipe on page 90).

PORK

Spareribs rank among the all-time favorite meats with back yard chefs. Ribs can be grilled or spitted, cut in pieces, or left whole as fancy dictates. The thing to remember is that all ribs, no matter how they're prepared, benefit from basting with a sauce of some character. Great though ribs may be, they are not the only part of a pig that does well on a barbecue. Fresh or smoked chops come off a fire as savory meats. So do roasts, whether left whole or boned and tied. Ham, surprising as it may seem, also is an excellent candidate. Not least, there are pork sausages of many sorts, including the good old-fashioned hot dog.

Basic Recipe:
Oven-barbecued Spareribs

Open or covered grill • Cooking time: About 1½ hours

Because ribs take up so much space on the grill, many cooks like to oven-cook them first, then reheat and glaze them on the barbecue. This method is especially good if you are trying to serve a large number of people. You can reheat and glaze the ribs in small batches, then put some more on the grill to heat while you eat the first ones.

Marinade (optional)
3½ to 4 pounds lean pork spareribs, cut in serving-size pieces
Baste (optional)

If you prepare a marinade (see Favorite Pork Marinades & Bastes, page 35), pour it over spareribs, cover them, and refrigerate for at least 4 hours or until next day.

Lift ribs from marinade and drain briefly (reserve marinade). Arrange ribs, fat-side-up, in a shallow roasting pan. Cook, uncovered, in a 350° oven for 1 hour and 15 minutes, basting occasionally with reserved marinade. Drain off excess fat.

When ready to barbecue, place ribs on lightly greased grill 4 to 6 inches above a solid bed of low-glowing coals. Cook, basting with reserved marinade or with a baste and turning ribs frequently, for 15 to 20 minutes or until crisp and well browned all over. Makes about 4 servings.

Basic Recipe:
Hot Dogs & Sausages

Open or covered grill • Cooking time: About 12 minutes

A barbecued hot dog wrapped in a bun can take on new dimensions when you substitute your own favorite selection of precooked sausages, breads, and condiments for the more standard ingredients. For example, you might choose long slender veal franks, smoky pork sausage links, garlic-flavored knackwurst, chicken and turkey franks, or a combination of these. If you use chorizo sausages, or others requiring precooking, simmer for 20 minutes, then drain before grilling. Allow ¼ to ½ pound of frankfurters or sausages per person.

Traditional hot dog buns may be the family favorite but sometimes it's fun to try something a little different. Warmed flour tortillas, crusty French rolls, onion rolls, or other breads like sliced rye or whole grain wheat make delicious wrappers for grilled sausages and franks. Serve them piled high with various condiments, if you wish, or as open-faced sandwiches.

Various types of mustards from plain to spicy hot are always good, but offer some of the following, too: catsup, chile salsa, horseradish, sliced onions and tomatoes, vegetable relishes, shredded cheeses, guacamole or sauerkraut.

2 pounds beef frankfurters or other sausages (see suggestions above)
16 to 20 hot dog buns, split and buttered, or other breads (suggestions precede)

Place frankfurters on lightly greased grill 4 to 6 inches above a solid bed of medium-glowing coals. Cook, turning often, for about 10 minutes or until done to your liking and heated throughout. Place buns, cut-side-down, around outside of grill to toast, if desired. Makes 8 to 10 servings.

Basic Recipe: Grilled Pork Chops

Open or covered grill • Cooking time: 15–20 minutes per side

Pork chops grilled slowly over coals acquire a smoky flavor typical of cured ham.

4 loin pork chops, cut 1 inch thick
Salt and pepper

Place chops on lightly greased grill 4 to 6 inches above a solid bed of medium-glowing coals. Cook, turning once, for 15 to 20 minutes on each side or until meat near bone is no longer pink when slashed. Season with salt and pepper to taste. Makes 4 servings.

Basic Recipe: Grilled Ham Steak

Open or covered grill • Cooking time: About 20 minutes

A thick, fully cooked, center cut ham slice takes less than 30 minutes to barbecue on the grill. Slice diagonally across the grain to serve 5 to 6 people.

Easy ham glaze (recipe follows)
1 center cut ham slice (about 1¾ lbs.), cut 1 inch thick

Prepare glaze; set aside. Place ham on lightly greased grill 4 to 6 inches above a solid bed of low-glowing coals. Cook, turning and basting occasionally with glaze, for about 20 minutes or until browned and hot. Makes 5 or 6 servings.

Easy ham glaze. Combine 3 tablespoons **honey,** 1 tablespoon *each* **Worcestershire** and **dry mustard,** ¾ teaspoon ground **ginger,** and dash of **pepper;** mix well and brush over ham slice as it cooks.

Favorite Pork Marinades & Bastes

Soy-flavored Marinade
Combine ½ cup *each* regular-strength **chicken broth** and **soy sauce**, ¼ cup **dry sherry** or Japanese sake, 6 tablespoons **sugar**, and 1 teaspoon **garlic** (minced or pressed). Pour over pork, cover, and refrigerate for at least 24 hours.

Savory Raisin Baste
Combine ½ cup finely chopped **raisins**, ¼ cup chopped **onion**, 1 clove **garlic** (minced or pressed), ½ cup *each* **catsup** and regular-strength **beef broth** or dry white wine, 3 tablespoons **salad oil**, 2 tablespoons **wine vinegar**, 1 tablespoon firmly packed **brown sugar**, 1 teaspoon *each* prepared **mustard** and **liquid smoke** (optional), ½ teaspoon **salt**, and ⅛ teaspoon **dill weed**. Simmer for 10 to 15 minutes. Makes about 1¾ cups.

Apricot Baste
Purée 1 can (about 9 oz.) undrained **apricots** or peaches. Combine with ¼ cup **catsup**, 3 tablespoons **lemon juice**, 2 tablespoons **salad oil** or melted butter, ½ teaspoon *each* **liquid smoke** (optional) and **salt**, and ⅛ teaspoon grated **lemon peel**. Simmer for 10 to 15 minutes. Makes 1½ cups.

Orange-glazed Ribs

Open or covered grill • Cooking time: 1½ hours

Orange marmalade and orange juice combine to give these ribs a delicious flavor and fine glaze.

3½ to 4 pounds lean pork spareribs, cut in serving-size pieces
½ cup orange marmalade
⅔ cup orange juice
⅓ cup Worcestershire
3 tablespoons lemon juice
¾ teaspoon *each* dry mustard and ground ginger
¼ teaspoon salt
⅛ teaspoon pepper
1 clove garlic, minced or pressed

Combine marmalade, orange juice, Worcestershire, lemon juice, mustard, ginger, salt, pepper, and garlic. Pour over spareribs; cover and refrigerate for at least 4 hours or until next day.

Lift ribs from marinade and drain briefly (reserve marinade). Arrange ribs, fat-side-up, in a

PLUM-FLAVORED PORK SPARERIBS (recipe above right) are slow-cooked to perfection, then served with foil-wrapped corn on the cob (recipe on page 90).

shallow roasting pan. Cook, uncovered, in a 350° oven for 1 hour and 15 minutes, basting frequently with reserved marinade. Drain off excess fat.

When ready to barbecue, place ribs on lightly greased grill 4 to 6 inches above a solid bed of low-glowing coals. Cook, turning and basting frequently with reserved marinade, for 15 to 20 minutes or until ribs are well browned and crisp. Makes about 4 servings.

Plum-flavored Ribs

Open or covered grill • Cooking time: About 1 hour

Here's a plum marinade that's excellent for pork spareribs, but you'll find it equally good with beef ribs or lamb riblets. *(Pictured on opposite page)*

3 tablespoons soy sauce
1 cup dry red wine
¼ cup *each* red wine vinegar and salad oil
⅓ cup plum jam
2 cloves garlic, minced or pressed
1 medium-size onion, finely chopped
½ teaspoon thyme leaves
8 pounds lean pork spareribs, left uncut in whole slabs

In a small pan over medium heat, combine soy, wine, vinegar, oil, jam, garlic, onion, and thyme. Stir until bubbling, then cool.

Put a large plastic bag in a rimmed baking pan. Place rib slabs in bag, pour in marinade, and twist-tie bag closed. Refrigerate for 4 hours or until next day, turning bag over occasionally.

Lift ribs from marinade and drain briefly (reserve marinade). Place on lightly greased grill 4 to 6 inches above a solid bed of low-glowing coals. Cook, turning and basting frequently with reserved marinade, for about 1 hour or until meat near bone is no longer pink when slashed. Cut into individual ribs to serve. Makes about 8 servings.

Garlic Spareribs

Spit-roasted • Cooking time: About 1½ hours

Uncut pork spareribs are threaded onto a barbecue spit and cooked over low-glowing coals for about 90 minutes.

4 cloves garlic, minced or pressed
1 cup *each* regular-strength chicken broth and orange marmalade
¼ cup *each* vinegar and catsup
About 6 pounds lean pork spareribs, left uncut in whole slabs

(Continued on next page)

Combine garlic, broth, marmalade, vinegar, and catsup. Put a large plastic bag in a rimmed baking pan. Place rib slabs in bag, pour in marinade, and twist-tie bag closed. Refrigerate until next day, turning bag over occasionally.

Arrange enough low-glowing coals to form a solid rectangular bed about 6 inches across and extending 3 to 4 inches beyond ends of ribs (see illustration, page 11). Coals should be about 2 inches behind an imaginary wall extending from spit to firebed. Place metal drip pan directly beneath and in front of spit.

Lift ribs from marinade and drain briefly (reserve marinade). Passing the spit through meaty sections, thread ribs back and forth in an s-shaped pattern. Position spit on barbecue and start motor. Cook, basting occasionally but sparingly with reserved marinade, for 1 to 1½ hours or until meat near bone is no longer pink when slashed. Every ½ hour add 5 or 6 briquets to fire, spacing them evenly, to maintain a constant temperature. Makes about 6 servings.

Easy Country-style Spareribs

Open or covered grill • Cooking time: 1–1¼ hours

First you cook these ribs on the grill, then finish them in a covered pan filled with barbecue sauce.

> 1 cup *each* catsup, water, and dry sherry
> ¼ cup Worcestershire
> 1 medium-size onion, sliced
> 1 large lemon, thinly sliced
> 1 clove garlic, minced or pressed
> 2 tablespoons butter or margarine
> 4 pounds lean country-style spareribs
>   Salt and pepper

In a 4-quart kettle that can be used on a barbecue grill, combine catsup, water, sherry, Worcestershire, onion, lemon, garlic, and butter. Bring to a boil, reduce heat, and simmer for 30 minutes.

Arrange ribs, fat-side-up, on lightly greased grill 4 to 6 inches above a solid bed of low-glowing coals. Baste lightly with sauce. Cook, turning oc-

casionally, for 1 hour to 1 hour and 20 minutes, or until meat near bone is no longer pink when slashed. Every ½ hour add 5 or 6 briquets to fire, spacing them evenly, to maintain a constant temperature.

Reheat remaining barbecue sauce by placing kettle on grill. As ribs cook, remove them from grill, cut into serving-size pieces, and place in kettle. Cover and simmer for 20 to 30 minutes longer. Spoon sauce over pieces to serve. Season with salt and pepper. Makes about 6 servings.

Gingered Spareribs

Open or covered grill • Cooking time: About 2 hours

You baste the spareribs with a spicy tomato sauce. Sprinkle with finely chopped candied ginger.

> 1 can (8 oz.) tomato sauce
> 1 can (about 1 lb.) tomato purée
> ¼ cup *each* wine vinegar and firmly packed
>   brown sugar
> 1 tablespoon Worcestershire
> 1 or 2 lemon slices
> 1 medium-size onion, finely chopped
> 1 clove garlic, minced or pressed
> 1 teaspoon salt
> ½ teaspoon *each* chili powder, celery salt,
>   and dry mustard
> ⅛ teaspoon pepper
> 6 pounds lean country-style spareribs
> 2 tablespoons very finely chopped candied
>   ginger

In a 2-quart pan, combine tomato sauce, purée, vinegar, sugar, Worcestershire, lemon, onion, garlic, salt, chili powder, celery salt, mustard, and pepper. Bring to a boil, reduce heat, cover, and simmer for 20 minutes, stirring occasionally.

Arrange ribs on lightly greased grill 4 to 6 inches above a solid bed of low-glowing coals. Cook, turning often and basting occasionally with sauce, for about 1½ hours or until meat near bone is no longer pink when slashed. Every ½ hour add 5 or 6 briquets to fire, spacing them evenly to maintain a constant temperature. Before serving, sprinkle with ginger. Makes about 8 servings.

Honey-glazed Ribs

Covered grill • Cooking time: About 1½ hours

You'll need a covered barbecue for this recipe. By adding some soaked hickory chips to the fire, you'll increase the smoky flavor of the ribs.

  ¼ **cup soy sauce**
  1 **teaspoon pepper**
  4 **tablespoons honey**
  ¼ **cup dry sherry**
  6 **pounds lean pork spareribs, left uncut in whole slabs**

Combine soy, pepper, honey, and sherry. Pour over ribs and allow to stand for 30 minutes to 1 hour, turning frequently. Lift ribs from marinade and drain briefly. Allow them to dry in the air for at least 1 hour—surface should have a dry feeling.

Bank about 20 low-glowing coals on each side of fire grill and place a metal drip pan in center. Scatter hickory chips (presoak chips in water for 30 minutes) over coals, if desired. Place grill 4 to 6 inches above drip pan; grease grill lightly.

Place ribs on grill directly over drip pan. Cover barbecue and adjust dampers according to manufacturer's directions.

Cook, turning occasionally and basting during last ½ hour with reserved marinade, for about 1½ hours or until meat near bone is no longer pink when slashed. Add 5 or 6 briquets to each side of fire every ½ hour to maintain a constant temperature. Makes about 6 servings.

Pineapple Spareribs

Open or covered grill • Cooking time: About 1 hour

A sweet and sour pineapple baste flavors these ribs. Since they're precooked, they need only be reheated and given a final basting.

 10 **pounds lean pork spareribs, cut in serving-size pieces**
    Boiling water
 12 **whole black peppers**
  6 **whole cloves**
  2 **bay leaves**
  2 **cloves garlic**
    Sweet and sour glaze (recipe follows)

Place ribs in a large deep kettle with enough boiling water to cover them completely. Add peppers, cloves, bay leaves, and garlic. Reduce heat and simmer for 30 minutes. Then drain, cover, and refrigerate until next day, if desired.

When ready to barbecue, arrange ribs on lightly greased grill 4 to 6 inches above a solid bed of low-glowing coals. Cook, turning frequently and basting often with glaze, for about 30 minutes or until meat near bone is no longer pink when slashed. Makes 10 to 12 servings.

Sweet and sour glaze. In a saucepan, combine 1 can (8½ oz.) crushed **pineapple,** ¾ cup regular-strength **chicken broth** or dry white wine, 3 tablespoons **white wine vinegar,** 2 tablespoons **salad oil,** 1 tablespoon **soy sauce,** 1 tablespoon firmly packed **brown sugar,** 1 teaspoon **lemon juice,** and ½ teaspoon **garlic salt.** Bring to a boil; reduce heat and simmer for 10 to 15 minutes.

Sherry-flavored Ham for a Crowd

Covered grill • Cooking time: About 3 hours

We used a large, fully cooked, bone-in ham for this recipe that serves about 25. If you wish, add soaked hickory chips to the coals during the last hour of cooking to give the ham a hickory-smoked flavor.

 12 **to 14-pound fully cooked ham**
  3 **tablespoons prepared mustard**
  2 **teaspoons ground cloves**
  1 **cup dry sherry or orange juice**

With a sharp knife, score top of ham in a crisscross pattern, cutting about ¼ inch deep. Rub surface with mustard; sprinkle with cloves.

Bank about 20 medium-glowing coals on each side of fire grill and place a metal drip pan in center. Place grill 4 to 6 inches above drip pan; grease grill lightly. Insert meat thermometer into center of thickest portion of ham but not touching bone.

Place ham on grill directly over drip pan. Cover barbecue and adjust dampers according to manufacturer's directions. Cook for about 2½ hours, adding 5 or 6 briquets on each side of fire every ½ hour to maintain a constant temperature.

After 2½ hours, add hickory chips (presoak chips in water for 30 minutes) to the fire, if you wish, and begin basting every 15 minutes with sherry. Cook until meat thermometer registers 135° (about 3 to 3½ hours total). Makes about 25 servings.

Ham Steak & Cantaloupe

Open or covered grill • Cooking time: 16–20 minutes

Both the wedges of ripe cantaloupe and the ham slice are generously brushed with a delicious honey-flavored baste as they cook.

> 2 tablespoons melted butter or margarine
> 3 tablespoons honey
> ¼ cup lime juice
>   Nutmeg
> 1 center cut fully cooked ham slice (about 2½ lbs.), cut 1 to 1½ inches thick
> 1 large cantaloupe

In a small pan, combine butter, honey, lime juice, and dash of nutmeg. Heat, stirring until blended; set aside but reheat before using.

Slash outer layer of fat (at 2-inch intervals) on ham slice to prevent curling. Brush both sides of ham steak with basting sauce. Place on lightly greased grill 4 to 6 inches above a solid bed of medium-glowing coals. Cook, turning occasionally and basting frequently with reserved basting sauce, for 16 to 20 minutes.

Meanwhile, cut cantaloupe into 6 wedges, remove seeds, then peel. About 10 minutes before ham is done, brush melon with basting sauce and place on grill. Cook fruit, turning and basting often, for 8 to 10 minutes or until glazed and lightly browned on all sides. To serve, arrange ham and fruit on carving board. Cut meat across the grain in thin, slanting slices. Makes about 6 servings.

Spicy Ham Steak

Open or covered grill • Cooking time: About 20 minutes

A fruity baste flavored with clove and pineapple penetrates this thick ham steak. You can barbecue it at home or bring it along, still marinating, to your favorite picnic site.

> ¼ cup melted butter or margarine
> 1 cup *each* dry sherry and pineapple juice
> 2 teaspoons *each* ground cloves and paprika
> ¼ teaspoon *each* dry mustard and firmly packed brown sugar
> 1 clove garlic, minced or pressed
> 1 center cut ham slice (about 1¾ lbs.), cut 1 inch thick

Combine butter, sherry, pineapple juice, cloves, paprika, mustard, sugar, and garlic. Pour over ham, cover, and refrigerate for at least 3 hours.

Lift ham from marinade and drain briefly (reserve marinade). Place ham on lightly greased grill 4 to 6 inches above a solid bed of low-glowing coals. Cook, turning and basting frequently, for about 20 minutes or until browned and hot. Makes about 5 or 6 servings.

Grilled Ham Slices

Open or covered grill • Cooking time: 3–5 minutes per side

A simple marinade that later becomes the serving sauce, transforms ordinary canned ham into something special.

> ½ cup *each* catsup, water, and salad oil
> 4 cloves garlic, minced or pressed
> 1 can (3 lbs.) fully cooked ham, cut in ¾-inch slices

Combine catsup, water, oil, and garlic. Place ham slices in shallow pan, pour over marinade, cover, and refrigerate for 4 hours or until next day, turning occasionally.

Lift slices from marinade and drain briefly. Pour marinade through a wire strainer into a small pan; set aside. Place ham slices on lightly greased grill 4 to 6 inches above a solid bed of low-glowing coals. Cook for 3 to 5 minutes on each side or until browned and hot. Heat marinade to serve as a sauce. Makes about 8 servings.

Sweet & Sour Pork Chops

Open or covered grill • Cooking time: 10 minutes

Smoked pork chops, carrots, and apple rings all cook together quickly in this festive barbecue dinner. The sweet and sour baste that glazes the meat, fruit, and vegetables is also used in the sauce that is spooned over individual portions. *(Pictured on opposite page)*

> ½ cup *each* sugar and wine vinegar
> 2 teaspoons *each* soy sauce and dry sherry
> ¼ cup catsup
>   Sweet and sour sauce (recipe follows)
> 4 smoked pork chops (about 3 lbs.), cut 1 inch thick
> 8 to 10 whole small carrots, peeled and cooked
> 4 large apples, unpeeled and cut horizontally into 1-inch-thick slices

Combine sugar, vinegar, soy, sherry, and catsup. Reserve ½ cup for sweet and sour sauce; use remainder as baste.

(Continued on page 43)

BASTED OFTEN, thick smoked pork chops broil on indoor barbecue grill alongside whole carrots and apple rounds. (Recipe above)

Breakfast from the Grill

A fine way to take advantage of good weather or a leisurely morning is to start the day with a special outdoor breakfast. Because many barbecue units have a large grill surface—from 18 to 40 inches across —practically any type of heat-resistant skillet or pan (don't forget the versatile wok) can be used to prepare food. Bacon and eggs, French toast, pancakes, even hash brown potatoes are handled easily on the barbecue when cooked over a solid bed of medium or low-glowing coals.

Lollipop Link Sausage Skewers

Skewer-cooked • Cooking time: 8–10 minutes

Two link sausages, bent in a spiral shape, are fastened with a thin wooden skewer (6 to 8 inches long) to make what appears to be a "sausage lollipop." Parboil the sausages first, then brown on the grill when ready to serve.

> 1 pound mild Italian or other pork link sausage (make sure connective sausage casing or "link" is intact)

Bend 2 or 3 link sausages in a spiral shape and spear with a thin, wooden skewer. Place skewered sausages in a large pan, cover with water, and bring to boiling. Remove from heat and allow to stand for 10 minutes. Drain and set aside.

Place precooked sausages on lightly greased grill 4 to 6 inches above a solid bed of medium-glowing coals. Cook, turning occasionally, for 8 to 10 minutes or until well browned all over. Makes 4 to 6 servings.

Foil-wrapped Sweet Rolls or Coffee Cake

Open or covered grill • Cooking time: 8–10 minutes

Frozen, ready-made sweet rolls or coffee cake that come packaged in an aluminum foil pan are perfect for heating outdoors on the barbecue. You'll have to allow them time to defrost (about 45 minutes) before placing on the grill.

> 1 package (about 10½ oz.) frozen sweet rolls or coffee cake, completely thawed

Remove package lid from sweet rolls or coffee cake. If desired (it makes for easier handling later on), lift rolls or cake out of foil pan and cut into serving-size pieces while still frozen. Then return to foil pan.

Place pan on heavy-duty foil and loosely wrap, completely enclosing pan in foil. Bank about 10 low-glowing coals on each side of fire grill and place cooking grill 4 to 6 inches above coals. Set foil-wrapped pan in center of grill so that no part is directly over coals. Cook, rotating pan occasionally to guarantee even heating, for about 8 to 10 minutes. Makes about 6 servings.

Sausage & Fruit Skewers

Skewer-cooked • Cooking time: 5–7 minutes

Thin wooden skewers (6 to 8 inches long) of fruit and precooked sausage are basted with a sauce of honey and lime.

> 2 pounds mild Italian pork sausage
> 1 large pineapple
> 1 large cantaloupe
> Honey-lime sauce (recipe follows)

Place sausage in a wide frying pan and add water to cover. Bring water to boiling, then reduce heat, cover, and simmer gently for 20 minutes; drain and set aside. (If done ahead, cook, then wrap and refrigerate.) Peel and core pineapple; cut into ¾ inch cubes; set aside. Cut cantaloupe in half, peel and scoop out and discard seeds. Cut into ¾ inch cubes. Prepare honey-lime sauce.

Group pineapple, cantaloupe, and sausage separately on a large platter. Skewer whole sausages lengthwise along with pieces of fruit; or, cut sausages into chunks and alternately thread on skewers with fruit.

Brush honey-lime sauce on skewered sausage and fruit and place on lightly greased grill 4 to 6 inches above a solid bed of glowing coals. Cook, turning often and basting with sauce, for 5 to 7 minutes or just until brown on all sides. Makes about 6 servings.

Honey-lime sauce. In a small serving dish, stir together ½ cup **lime juice** and 3 tablespoons **honey.** Makes about ⅔ cup.

Chive Omelet for Six

Open or covered grill • Cooking time: About 15 minutes

A simple omelet, in this case made with chives, can be glorified a number of different ways. Try adding shredded cheese, sautéed mushrooms, and chopped onions; or bits of cooked sausage, ham, or bacon.

- 8 eggs, separated
- 2 tablespoons all-purpose flour
- 3 tablespoons milk
- 2 teaspoons chopped chives
- ½ teaspoon *each* salt and onion salt
- ¼ teaspoon Worcestershire
  - Dash pepper
  - Butter

Beat egg yolks until creamy; gradually beat in flour, milk, chives, salt, onion salt, Worcestershire, and pepper. Beat egg whites until stiff but not dry. Fold thoroughly but gently into yolk mixture. Spoon into a well-buttered, shallow 2-quart casserole that's made of heavy metal or is heat-resistant.

Bank about 20 medium-glowing coals on each side of fire grill and place cooking grill 4 to 6 inches above coals. Place casserole on grill so that no part of pan is directly over coals. Cover barbecue and adjust dampers according to manufacturer's directions. (Make a tent of foil to enclose omelet if cooking on an open grill.)

Cook for 13 to 15 minutes or until top is golden brown. Serve immediately. Makes 6 servings.

Bacon Corn Muffins

Open or covered grill • Cooking time: About 15 minutes

Bacon bits flavor these traditional corn muffins. Serve them hot from the grill.

- 6 strips bacon
- 1 cup all-purpose flour
- 2 teaspoons baking powder
- ½ teaspoon *each* salt and soda
- ⅓ cup sugar
- 1 cup *each* yellow cornmeal and buttermilk
- 1 egg

In a wide frying pan over medium-high heat, cook bacon until browned; drain (reserve 2 tablespoons of the drippings), and coarsely chop. Combine flour with baking powder, salt, soda, and sugar. Sift into a bowl containing cornmeal. Mix well.

To buttermilk, add egg and reserved bacon drippings; beat lightly. Stir chopped bacon (reserve about 1 tablespoon for topping) and buttermilk mixture into dry ingredients *just* until adequately combined.

Line muffin pan with paper muffin cups. Fill ⅔ of each cup with batter; sprinkle reserved bacon over tops. Bank about 20 glowing coals on each side of fire grill and place cooking grill 4 to 6 inches above coals. Set muffin pan in center of grill so that no part is directly over coals. Cook for about 12 minutes (10 minutes in a covered barbecue), then check for doneness. Continue checking every minute or so as glowing coals bake muffins quickly. Makes 9 muffins.

Place chops, carrots, and apple slices on lightly greased grill 4 to 6 inches above a solid bed of low-glowing coals. Cook, turning frequently and basting with reserved sauce, for about 10 minutes or until meat, carrots, and apple are browned and hot. Serve with heated sweet and sour sauce. Makes 4 servings.

Sweet and sour sauce. Gradually stir ⅔ cup regular-strength **chicken broth** into 1 tablespoon **cornstarch** until blended; stir in the ½ cup reserved baste mixture. In a frying pan over medium-high heat, warm 1 tablespoon **salad oil.** Add 1 clove **garlic** (minced or pressed) and 1 large **onion** (thinly sliced). Cook, stirring constantly, until onion is limp. Add cornstarch-baste mixture and cook, stirring, until thickened.

Savory Pork Balls with Apples

Skewer-cooked • Cooking time: 15–20 minutes

Skewers of savory ground pork balls and apple quarters, with ripples of bacon in between, offer a winning combination for the barbecue.

1½ pounds lean ground pork
1 egg
⅓ cup *each* fine dry bread crumbs and finely chopped onion
2 tablespoons apple juice
½ teaspoon *each* salt and ground ginger
¼ teaspoon *each* ground sage and pepper
2 large Golden Delicious apples, cored and quartered
8 strips bacon

Combine pork, egg, bread crumbs, onion, apple juice, salt, ginger, sage, and pepper. Divide into 16 equal portions; shape each into a ball.

To assemble on skewers (you'll need 4 sturdy metal ones), pierce one end of a bacon strip with a skewer, then push on a pork ball, pierce bacon again, and add an apple quarter. Pierce bacon again, push on another pork ball, and then pierce bacon end; the bacon forms S-curves around the meat and apple. Repeat until each skewer has 2 bacon strips, 4 pork balls, and 2 apple quarters all spaced loosely so bacon will brown evenly.

Place on lightly greased grill 4 to 6 inches above a solid bed of low-glowing coals. Cook, turning gently as needed to brown evenly, for 15 to 20 minutes or until bacon is crisp and pork is no longer pink when slashed. Makes 4 servings.

FESTIVE OCCASIONS call for festive foods. What captures the appetites of hungry party-goers better than grilled hot dogs with all the trimmings? (Recipe on page 33)

Pork Sausage Logs

Open or covered grill • Cooking time: About 15 minutes

Ground pork and ground beef are mixed together, seasoned, and shaped into logs before they are grilled over hot coals. Serve them plain or with warmed slices of bread or tortillas.

1 pound *each* lean ground beef and ground pork
2 cloves garlic, minced or pressed
1¼ teaspoon salt
¼ teaspoon pepper
4 teaspoons *each* paprika and olive oil
⅓ cup lightly packed minced parsley

Mix ground meats, garlic, salt, pepper, paprika, oil, and parsley until well blended. Using about 2 tablespoons of the mixture for each, shape into logs about 2½ inches long. Cover and chill until firm (about 20 minutes).

Place on lightly greased grill 4 to 6 inches above a solid bed of medium-glowing coals. Cook, turning occasionally, for 12 to 15 minutes or until well browned on all sides and meat is no longer pink when slashed. Makes about 3 dozen sausage logs.

Pork Skewers & Peaches

Skewer-cooked • Cooking time: About 12 minutes

Barbecue these peach-flavored kebabs and serve them with fresh peach slices. You can refrigerate the meat in marinade for several hours or a day ahead, if you like.

1 large peach or 1 jar (7 oz.) strained peaches for infants
¼ cup *each* honey, lemon juice, salad oil, and soy sauce
1 small onion, finely chopped
1 clove garlic, minced or pressed
⅛ teaspoon ground ginger
2½ to 3 pounds lean boneless pork (leg or shoulder), cut into 1½ inch pieces
4 firm ripe peaches, peeled, pitted, and halved

Peel and pit large peach. Whirl in a blender or pour through a strainer; you should have about ½ cup purée. Combine with honey, lemon juice, oil, soy, onion, garlic, and ginger. Pour over meat, cover, and refrigerate for 2 hours or until next day.

Lift meat from marinade and drain briefly (reserve marinade). Divide meat evenly among sturdy metal skewers. Cut peach halves into thick slices and thread onto thin wooden or metal skew-

(Continued on page 45)

Variety Meats

Variety or organ meats are rarely considered for barbecuing, yet their flavor and succulent texture make them an unusually tasty choice for any outdoor occasion. It's important not to overcook them.

Grilled Kidneys

Open grill • Cooking time: 5–15 minutes

Beef, veal, lamb, and pork kidneys may be successfully grilled over charcoal. They take from 5 to 15 minutes to cook, depending on the size.

1 pound beef, veal, lamb, or pork kidneys
Melted butter or margarine
Salt and pepper

Split kidneys and remove fat and connective tissue. Brush with melted butter (seasoned, if you wish) and place on lightly greased grill 4 to 6 inches above a solid bed of medium-glowing coals. Cook, turning frequently, for 5 to 15 minutes, depending on size. Kidneys are done when browned on the outside but still juicy and pink on the inside. Season with salt and pepper to taste. Slice to serve. Makes about 4 servings.

Liver, Bacon & Onion Skewers

Skewer-cooked • Cooking time: About 8 minutes

The familiar flavor combination of liver, bacon, and onions takes on a lively new dimension when served from a skewer. Partially cook the bacon strips first.

12 strips bacon
2 pounds beef liver, sliced ½-inch thick
Salt and pepper
2 cans (8 oz. *each*) small whole onions, drained

Partially cook bacon until it starts to brown but is still limp; drain on paper towels. Cut liver into 1-inch pieces and sprinkle lightly with salt and pepper to taste.

To prepare 6 skewers, pierce one end of a bacon strip with a skewer, then thread on a piece of liver and an onion. Cover with the bacon strip, pierce it again; add another strip of bacon, and another piece of liver and an onion, and add the other end of the bacon strip, so that the bacon forms S-curves around meat and onions. Repeat the process, using 2 strips of bacon for each skewer.

Place on lightly greased grill 4 to 6 inches above a solid bed of medium-glowing coals. Cook, turning often, for 6 to 8 minutes or until bacon is crisp and liver is cooked but still slightly pink inside. Makes 6 servings.

Glazed Beef Tongue

Covered grill • Cooking time: About 1 hour

First you simmer the beef tongue until almost tender (this can be done a day ahead) and then finish cooking it in a covered barbecue for smoky flavor.

1 fresh beef tongue (3 to 4 lbs.)
1 large onion, chopped
Water
1 cup buttermilk
1 tablespoon each Dijon-style mustard and honey
⅛ teaspoon pepper

Place tongue and onion in a Dutch oven; cover with water. Cover pan and simmer for about 2½ hours or until almost tender. Let cool in broth. Cover and refrigerate overnight, if desired.

In a small pan, combine buttermilk, mustard, honey, and pepper. Heat just until honey is dissolved. When meat is cool, remove skin and fat. (If refrigerated, let stand at room temperature for several hours before removing skin and fat.)

Bank about 20 low-glowing coals on each side of fire grill and place a metal drip pan in center. Adjust cooking grill so that surface is 4 to 6 inches above drip pan; grease grill lightly. Place tongue on grill directly over drip pan; cover barbecue and adjust dampers according to manufacturer's directions. Cook, basting frequently with buttermilk baste, for about 1 hour or until meat is glazed and tender. Makes 8 to 10 servings.

...Pork Skewers & Peaches (cont'd.)

ers. Brush skewered meat with reserved marinade and place on lightly greased grill 4 to 6 inches above a solid bed of low-glowing coals. Cook, turning and basting frequently with marinade, for 10 to 12 minutes or until pork is no longer pink when slashed. After meat has cooked for about 7 minutes, brush skewered peaches with marinade, place on grill, and cook, turning occasionally, for about 4 minutes. Makes 6 to 8 servings.

Spicy Pork Tenderloin

Open or covered grill • Cooking time: 30–60 minutes

You can use either a whole pork tenderloin or thick loin chops. The spicy flavor comes from a combination of chili powder, mustard, and honey.

¼ cup *each* prepared mustard and honey
¼ teaspoon *each* salt and chili powder
2½ to 3-pound pork tenderloin (or 4 to 6 loin chops, cut 1 inch thick)

Combine mustard, honey, salt, and chili powder. Spoon over pork, cover, and refrigerate for 4 hours or until next day.

Lift meat from marinade and drain briefly (reserve marinade). Place on lightly greased grill 4 to 6 inches above a solid bed of glowing coals. (If using chops, put thickest ones on first.) Cook, turning and basting occasionally for 45 to 60 minutes for tenderloin (30 to 40 minutes for chops) or until meat is no longer pink in center when slashed. To serve, cut meat across the grain in thin, slanting slices. Makes 4 to 6 servings.

Pork Loin with Melon Rings

Covered grill • Cooking time: About 2 hours

Thick slices of smoked pork atop grilled cantaloupe rings are garnished with a dollop of whipped cream cheese and chives.

2 packages (3 oz. *each*) cream cheese with chives, at room temperature
½ cup whipping cream
4-pound pork loin roast, boned and tied
2 tablespoons melted butter or margarine
2 large cantaloupes, peeled, seeded and cut in ½-inch-thick slices

Beat cream cheese and cream until fluffy; cover and refrigerate until ready to use.

Bank about 20 low-glowing coals on each side of fire grill and place a metal drip pan in center. Place grill 4 to 6 inches above drip pan; grease grill lightly. Insert meat thermometer into thickest portion of meat.

Place pork on grill directly over drip pan. Cover barbecue and adjust dampers according to manufacturer's directions. Cook for about 2 hours or until meat thermometer registers 170°. Add 5 or 6 briquets on each side of fire every ½ hour to maintain a constant temperature.

When roast is cooked, transfer to a warm platter. Brush both sides of cantaloupe rings with melted butter and place on grill directly over coals. Cook, turning once, for 3 to 4 minutes on each side or until warm.

To serve, place a slice of pork atop a melon ring and garnish with a dollop of whipped cheese sauce. Makes 8 to 10 servings.

Pork Shoulder Roast

Covered grill • Cooking time: 3–3½ hours

The rich flavor of this pork roast is tempered by a slightly sweet and spicy fruit juice marinade that can also be thickened to use as a sauce.

1 pork shoulder roast (about 5 lbs.), boned and tied
2 cups cranberry-apple juice
¼ teaspoon cinnamon
½ teaspoon chili powder
1 teaspoon instant minced onion
⅛ teaspoon pepper
2 teaspoons cornstarch (optional)

Place roast in a deep bowl. Combine juice, cinnamon, chili powder, onion, and pepper. Pour over meat, cover, and refrigerate for 2 to 4 hours.

Bank about 20 glowing coals on each side of fire grill and place a metal drip pan in center. Place grill 4 to 6 inches above drip pan; grease grill lightly.

Lift pork from marinade and drain briefly (reserve marinade). Insert a meat thermometer into center of roast. Reserve 1 cup of the marinade for the sauce, if desired. Place meat on grill directly over drip pan, cover barbecue and adjust dampers according to manufacturer's directions. Cook, basting every ½ hour with remaining marinade, for 3 to 3½ hours or until meat thermometer registers 175°. Add 5 or 6 briquets on each side of fire every ½ hour to maintain a constant temperature.

If you prepare the sauce, blend cornstarch into part of the 1 cup of reserved marinade. Stir until smooth, then add remaining marinade and cook over medium heat, stirring constantly, until clear and thickened. When ready to serve, pass sauce to spoon over cooked sliced meat. Makes 8 servings.

Venezuelan Pork Butt

Open or covered grill • Cooking time: 2–2½ hours

Fresh pork butt, boned and butterflied, resembles a compact rectangular steak about 1½ inches thick.

    1 large onion, coarsely chopped
    1 can (4 oz.) pimento, drained and chopped
    2 cloves garlic, minced or pressed
    ⅓ cup chopped parsley
    ½ cup white vinegar
    ¼ cup salad oil
    ¼ teaspoon pepper
    1 pork butt (about 6 lbs.), boned and
       butterflied
      Salt

Combine onion, pimento, garlic, parsley, vinegar, oil, and pepper. Set aside. With a knife, score top of meat in a crisscross pattern, cutting about ½ inch deep. Place meat in dish, pour over marinade, cover, and let stand for 2 hours.

Lift meat from marinade and drain briefly, scraping off vegetable bits (reserve marinade). Place on lightly greased grill 4 to 6 inches above a solid bed of low-glowing coals. Cook, turning and basting occasionally with reserved marinade, for about 2 hours or until meat thermometer inserted in center of thickest portion registers 170°. Add 5 or 6 briquets every ½ hour to fire to maintain a constant temperature.

Cut meat across the grain in thin, slanting slices; salt to taste. Heat remaining marinade for a sauce. Makes 10 to 12 servings.

Spit-roasted Leg of Pork

Spit-roasted • Cooking time: About 6 hours

A rolled roast made from a whole leg of pork (about 12 lbs.) is quite an impressive sight as it spit-roasts to a crusty brown color in about 6 hours.

    2 cups applesauce
    ¾ cup dry white wine
    ½ cup soy sauce
    2 tablespoons salad oil
    1 cup chopped onion
    1 clove garlic, minced or pressed
    1 teaspoon ground ginger
    1 leg of pork (about 12 lbs.), boned
      and rolled

Combine 1 cup of the applesauce with wine, soy, oil, onion, garlic, and ginger. Put roast into a large plastic bag, pour in marinade, and twist-tie bag closed. Refrigerate for 2 to 4 hours or until next day.

Arrange enough low-glowing coals to form a solid rectangular bed about 6 inches across and extending 3 to 4 inches beyond ends of meat (see illustration page 11). Coals should be about 2 inches behind an imaginary wall extending from spit to firebed. Place metal drip pan directly beneath and in front of spit.

Lift meat from marinade and drain briefly (reserve marinade). Run spit through exact center of roast — the weight of the roast must be evenly distributed around the spit or it will drag against the motor. Insert spit forks and tighten with pliers; position spit on barbecue and start motor.

Cook, basting occasionally during the last hour with reserved marinade, for about 6 hours or until meat thermometer inserted in thickest portion but not touching spit registers 170°. Every ½ hour add 5 or 6 briquets to fire, spacing them evenly, to maintain a constant temperature. Combine remaining marinade with remaining applesauce and heat as sauce. Makes 12 to 16 servings.

Apple-glazed Pork Roast

Covered grill • Cooking time: About 2½ hours

Apple juice, soy sauce, and ginger combine in this marinade to give a beautiful golden brown glaze and teriyakilike flavor to the roast.

    3½ to 4-pound pork loin roast
    1 cup apple juice
    3 tablespoons soy sauce
    1 clove garlic, minced or pressed
    ¼ teaspoon ground ginger
    1½ teaspoons *each* cornstarch and water

Bank about 20 medium-glowing coals on each side of fire grill and place a metal drip pan in center. Place grill 4 to 6 inches above drip pan; grease grill lightly. Place pork on grill, fat-side-up, directly over drip pan. Cover barbecue and adjust dampers according to manufacturer's directions.

Combine apple juice, soy, garlic, and ginger. After meat has cooked for 1 hour, baste with mixture. Cover barbecue and cook, basting often, for 1½ hours longer or until meat thermometer inserted in thickest portion but not touching bone registers 170°. Add 5 or 6 briquets to each side of the fire every ½ hour to maintain a constant temperature. To make gravy, skim fat from drippings in drip pan; combine cornstarch and water, then stir into drippings. Cook, stirring constantly, until thickened. Makes about 6 servings.

FOIL-WRAPPED VEGETABLES
include (clockwise from top)
squash spears with brown sugar, peas
with mushrooms, parsleyed new potatoes,
asparagus with pine nuts, lemony carrots,
whole artichokes, almond-topped green
beans, and zucchini-tomato casserole.
(Recipes on pages 89 and 90)

LAMB

For many outdoor chefs, the tender, juicy meat of spring
lamb has no rival when it comes to barbecuing.
The flavorful meat combines well with many other foods.
Lean chunks from the shoulder or leg can be threaded
on skewers with pieces of fruit or vegetables, or both. Well-
marinated chops or steaks cook quickly over a hot fire,
yet remain flavorful and tender. For the grand occasion,
whole legs can be boned and butterflied and
slow-cooked with herb bastes.

Basic Recipe: Lamb Shish Kebab

Skewer-cooked • Cooking time: 20–25 minutes

Among the classic uses of lamb in barbecue cooking are shish kebabs and their skewered relatives.

The basic recipe for skewer-cooked lamb calls for 1½-inch cubes of lean meat (either shoulder or leg) marinated for 2 to 4 hours, then grilled quickly on an open or covered grill until browned. Cooking times for smaller cubes appear at the end of the recipe. You may, if you like, skewer vegetables or chunks of fruit along with the lamb.

A simple marinade combines lemon juice and olive oil plus a variety of seasonings. *(Pictured on page 50)*

> 2 pounds boneless lean lamb (shoulder or leg), cut into 1½-inch cubes
> ⅓ cup olive oil or salad oil
> 3 tablespoons lemon juice
> 1 large onion, finely chopped
> 2 bay leaves
> 2 teaspoons oregano leaves
> ½ teaspoon pepper

Place cubes of lamb in a bowl. In another bowl, combine oil, lemon juice, onion, bay leaves, oregano, and pepper; pour over lamb cubes. Cover and refrigerate for 2 to 4 hours.

Lift lamb from marinade and drain briefly (reserve marinade). Divide meat evenly among sturdy metal skewers and place on a lightly greased grill 4 to 6 inches above a solid bed of glowing coals. Cook, turning and basting with reserved marinade, for 20 to 25 minutes or until lamb is well browned on all sides but still pink in center when slashed. (For ¾-inch cubes, cook 12 to 15 minutes; for 1-inch cubes, 15 to 20 minutes.) Makes about 6 servings.

Basic Recipe: Leg of Lamb on a Covered Grill

Covered grill • Cooking time: About 2 hours

If you wish, marinate this whole leg in an onion-flavored sauce before cooking. Use soaked hickory chips or freshly cut fruit wood on the fire if you enjoy a smoky flavor.

> 1 bone-in leg of lamb (about 6 lbs.)
> Onion-flavored marinade (recipe follows)

Bank about 20 medium-glowing coals on each side of the fire grill and place a metal drip pan in center. Place grill 4 to 6 inches above drip pan; grease grill lightly.

Brush lamb with a baste (see Favorite Lamb Marinades & Bastes, page 51) or, if marinated, lift meat from marinade and drain briefly (reserve marinade). Place meat on grill, directly over drip pan. Cover barbecue and adjust dampers according to manufacturer's directions.

Cook, basting occasionally with reserved marinade, for about 2 hours or until meat thermometer inserted into thickest portion (but not touching bone) registers 145° for rare, 155° for medium. Add 5 or 6 briquets on each side of fire every ½ hour to maintain a constant temperature. Makes about 8 servings.

Onion-flavored marinade. Combine 2 thinly sliced, medium-size **onions,** ½ teaspoon **pepper,** ½ cup **dry sherry** or orange juice, 2 tablespoons **olive oil** or salad oil, 1 teaspoon **oregano leaves,** and ½ teaspoon **savory leaves.** Pour over lamb, cover, and refrigerate for at least 8 hours or until next day. Turn meat occasionally.

Basic Recipe: Spit-roasted Leg of Lamb

Spit-roasted • Cooking time: About 1½ hours

A traditional way to barbecue a leg of lamb—even the largest—is on a spit.

> 1 leg of lamb (about 6 lbs.)
> Marinade (optional)

Select about a 6-pound, bone-in leg of lamb with the shank bone and the aitchbone (pronounced *H-bone*) removed, and the roast tied. You'll end up with an irregular oval about 3 to 4 inches by 7 to 8 inches. One long straight bone will remain near center of roast for balancing meat.

Run spit through center of roast from thickest end, keeping length of leg parallel to spit; secure with spit forks and tighten with your fingers.

To test for balance, pick up spit at both ends and rotate in palms of hands. If one side drags downward, reposition spit a little more toward light side or add a balance weight pointed toward light side. (A very slight tendency to spin doesn't matter, as motor can overcome it.) When leg is balanced, tighten forks with pliers to be sure they do not loosen during cooking.

Arrange enough low-glowing coals to form a solid rectangular bed about 6 inches across and extending 3 to 4 inches beyond the ends of the meat (see illustration, page 11). Coals should be about 2 inches behind an imaginary wall extending from spit to firebed. Place metal drip pan directly beneath and in front of spit. Meatiest part of leg should be about 5 inches above surface of coals.

(Continued on page 51)

Since diameter of roast determines length of cooking time (a long, narrow roast with a small diameter will cook faster than a short, wide roast), insert a meat thermometer in thickest portion (but not touching bone or spit rod).

Place spit on barbecue and start motor. Cook, basting occasionally (see Favorite Lamb Marinades & Bastes, below), for about 1½ hours or until meat thermometer registers 145° to 150° for medium. Add 5 or 6 briquets every ½ hour, spacing them evenly to maintain a constant temperature. Makes 8 to 10 servings.

Favorite Lamb Marinades & Bastes

Getting variety into your lamb barbecues can be as simple as varying the baste or marinade (see page 14 for a discussion of the difference between the two). Here we present some favorite recipes for these versatile little sauces.

Easy Lamb Marinade

Combine ½ cup **dry sherry** or apple juice, ¼ cup **olive oil** or salad oil, 2 teaspoons *each* **salt** and **oregano leaves**, ½ teaspoon **pepper**, and 1 large **onion** (sliced). Pour over lamb, cover, and chill up to 4 hours.

Honey-Wine Marinade

Melt 2 tablespoons **butter** in a pan. Add 1 cup **dry white wine**, 2 tablespoons **wine vinegar**, ⅓ cup **honey**, 1 teaspoon fresh or dry chopped **mint**, 1 teaspoon **salt,** and 2 cloves **garlic** (minced or pressed). Pour over lamb chops, shanks, or breast, and marinate for as long as 4 hours. Use remaining marinade to baste lamb as it cooks.

Shish Kebab Marinade

Combine 1 can (6 oz.) **tomato paste**, ½ cup **olive oil** or salad oil, 1 cup **honey**, 1 cup **dry white wine**, ½ teaspoon *each* crushed **dry rosemary** and **oregano leaves**, 1 teaspoon **salt,** and 2 cloves **garlic** (minced or pressed). Pour over skewers of lamb cubes, cover, and marinate for about an hour. Drain briefly and cook kebabs, using remaining marinade as a baste.

Mediterranean Leg of Lamb Baste

Cut 4 cloves **garlic** into slivers; using a small pointed knife, slit meat and insert garlic pieces in

CLASSIC SKEWERED SHISH KEBAB
(recipe on page 49), with alternating cubes of lamb and colorful vegetables, is served on a bed of nut-studded rice.

several places. For baste, melt 4 tablespoons **butter** or margarine in a pan; add 3 tablespoons **lemon juice** and ½ teaspoon **oregano leaves.** Use to baste lamb occasionally as it cooks.

Parsley-Orange Baste

Combine ½ cup (¼ lb.) melted **butter** or margarine, 2 tablespoons grated **orange peel**, 2 tablespoons finely chopped **parsley,** and 2 tablespoons **honey.** Add ¼ cup **lemon juice** and ½ teaspoon **salt.** Brush baste on meat several times as it cooks.

Lamb Sosaties & Fruit Skewers

Skewer-cooked • Cooking time: 20–25 minutes

Although our recipe comes from South Africa, the spicy, sweet-and-sour marinade is probably of Malayan or Indonesian origin. Serve these lamb kebabs with skewers of fruit, grilled just long enough to be heated throughout.

>4 **pounds lean boneless lamb** (shoulder or leg), cut into 1½-inch cubes
>1½ **cups cider vinegar**
>3 **tablespoons apricot** or **pineapple jam**
>4½ **teaspoons** *each* **curry powder** and firmly packed **brown sugar**
>¼ **teaspoon pepper**
>4 **small, dried hot chile peppers,** crushed
>2 **medium-size onions,** thinly sliced
>3 **cloves garlic,** minced or pressed
>2 **bay leaves**
>About 6 cups **fruit** (apricot halves, fresh or canned; pineapple chunks, fresh or canned; cantaloupe chunks; canned spiced crabapples; or a mixture of these)

Place meat cubes in a bowl. In a pan, combine vinegar, jam, curry powder, sugar, pepper, chile peppers, onion, garlic, and bay leaves; bring to a boil. Remove from heat, cool, and pour mixture through a strainer onto meat cubes. Cover and refrigerate for 2 to 4 hours, stirring occasionally.

Lift meat from marinade and drain briefly (reserve marinade). Divide meat evenly among sturdy metal skewers and place on a lightly greased grill 4 to 6 inches above a solid bed of low-glowing coals. Cook, turning and basting frequently with reserved marinade, for 20 to 25 minutes or until lamb is well browned on all sides but still pink in center when slashed.

As lamb cooks, thread fruit onto additional skewers. After lamb has cooked for 15 minutes, place fruit skewers on edge of grill; baste with reserved marinade and turn until heated throughout. Makes about 10 servings.

Lamb Kebabs in Plum Sauce

Skewer-cooked • Cooking time: 20–25 minutes

Quickly made from canned plums, this sweet-and-tangy plum sauce makes a distinctive marinade for chunks of lamb and whole mushrooms.

    1 **can (1 lb.) whole purple plums**
    2 **tablespoons butter or margarine**
    1 **medium-size onion, chopped**
   ⅓ **cup firmly packed brown sugar**
   ¼ **cup tomato-based chili sauce**
    2 **tablespoons soy sauce**
    1 **teaspoon ground ginger**
    2 **teaspoons lemon juice**
    2 **pounds lean boneless lamb (shoulder or leg), cut into 1½-inch cubes**
   ½ **pound medium-size mushrooms**

Drain plums, reserving syrup. Remove pits, then whirl plums and syrup in a blender until puréed. Melt butter in a pan over medium heat; add onion and cook until limp. Stir in sugar, chili sauce, soy, ginger, lemon juice, and plum purée. Simmer, uncovered, for about 30 minutes or until slightly thickened, stirring occasionally. Let cool, then pour over lamb, cover, and refrigerate for 4 hours or until next day.

Remove meat from marinade and drain briefly (reserve marinade). Alternately thread meat and mushrooms onto 4 to 6 sturdy metal skewers.

Place skewers on a lighly greased grill 4 to 6 inches above a solid bed of low-glowing coals. Cook, turning occasionally, for 20 to 25 minutes or until lamb is well browned on all sides but still pink in center when slashed. During last 10 minutes, brush kebabs with plum sauce. Makes 4 to 6 servings.

Lamb Kebabs for 12

Skewer-cooked • Cooking time: 15–20 minutes

Herb-flavored lamb cubes alternate with green pepper and onion pieces in this simple shish kebab recipe that serves up to a dozen people.

   ½ **cup dry sherry or apple juice**
   ¼ **cup olive oil or salad oil**
    2 **teaspoons oregano leaves**
   ½ **teaspoon pepper**
    2 *each* **large onions and green peppers**
    4 **pounds lean boneless lamb (shoulder or leg), cut into 1½-inch cubes**

Combine sherry, oil, oregano, and pepper. Thinly slice 1 of the onions, add to mixture, and pour over lamb. Cover and refrigerate for 2 to 4 hours or until next day, stirring occasionally.

Lift meat from marinade and drain briefly (reserve marinade). Cut the remaining onion into eight wedges. Seed green peppers and cut into 16 pieces, each about 1½ inches square. Divide meat and vegetables equally and thread on to long metal skewers (using 4 or 5 lamb cubes, 2 pieces green pepper, and 1 piece onion on each).

Place skewers on a lightly greased grill 4 to 6 inches above a solid bed of glowing coals. Cook, turning and basting frequently with reserved marinade, for 15 to 20 minutes or until lamb is well browned on all sides but still pink in center when slashed. Makes about 12 servings.

Lamb Sandwich Buffet

Skewer-cooked • Cooking time: 12–15 minutes

Spicy lamb cubes, vegetables, and unflavored yogurt combine in warm Arab bread or warm soft flour tortillas for a whole-meal sandwich. Arab bread (also called pocket, peda, or pita bread) is available in most supermarkets or in Middle Eastern delicatessens. *(Pictured on page 55)*

   ½ **cup lemon juice**
   ¼ **cup olive oil or salad oil**
    1 **teaspoon** *each* **chopped fresh coriander (cilantro) and ground cumin**
   ½ **teaspoon** *each* **pepper, ground turmeric, and crushed red pepper**
    2 **pounds lean boneless lamb (shoulder or leg), cut into ¾-inch cubes**
    2 **large onions, thinly sliced and separated into rings**
    6 **Arab bread or 12 flour tortillas**
  12 **to 24 small romaine spears**
    3 **medium-size tomatoes, cut into thin wedges**
    1 **cup unflavored yogurt**

Combine lemon juice, oil, coriander, cumin, pepper, turmeric, and red pepper. Place lamb and onion in separate bowls. Pour ½ of marinade over lamb, the other ½ over onion. Cover and refrigerate meat and onion for 2 to 4 hours, stirring occasionally.

Lift meat from marinade and drain briefly (reserve marinade). Divide meat evenly among sturdy metal skewers and place on a lightly greased grill 4 to 6 inches above a solid bed of glowing coals. Cook, turning and basting frequently with reserved marinade, for 12 to 15 minutes or until lamb is well browned on all sides but still pink in center when slashed.

As meat cooks, stack Arab bread or tortillas on a sheet of aluminum foil. (Sprinkle a few drops of water on each tortilla.) Wrap tightly and place near edge of grill (not directly over coals) to warm for about 10 minutes; turn often.

To serve, lift onion from marinade with slotted spoon and place in a serving bowl. Cut Arab bread in halves (you should have 12 halves or pockets). In each pocket put 1 or 2 romaine spears, 5 or 6 lamb cubes, a spoonful of onion rings, tomato wedges, and a dollop of yogurt. Or roll lamb and other ingredients in warmed flour tortillas. Makes 12 sandwiches.

Lamb Cubes in Onion Juice

Skewer-cooked • Cooking time: 12–15 minutes

The distinctive flavor of this dish comes from the juice of onions. Add vegetables if you wish.

    2 pounds lean boneless lamb (shoulder or
        leg), cut into 1½-inch cubes
    2 medium-size onions, cut in chunks
    ½ cup salad oil
    1 bay leaf
    ½ teaspoon thyme leaves
    1 teaspoon salt
    ⅛ teaspoon rubbed sage
    3 whole black peppers, crushed
    1 cup dry sherry or dry red wine

Place lamb in a bowl. Grind onion in food chopper or processor, using finest blade, or whirl in blender until liquefied. Combine onion with oil, bay leaf, thyme, salt, sage, pepper, and sherry; pour over lamb. Cover and refrigerate for 2 to 4 hours or until next day, stirring occasionally.

Lift meat from marinade and drain briefly (reserve marinade). Divide meat equally among 6 sturdy metal skewers and place on a lightly greased grill 4 to 6 inches above a solid bed of glowing coals. Cook, turning and basting frequently with reserved marinade, for 12 to 15 minutes or until lamb is well browned on all sides but still pink in center. Makes 6 servings.

Ground Lamb Kebabs with Pineapple

Skewer-cooked • Cooking time: 5–10 minutes

Spicy ground lamb balls grill alongside slices of pineapple. Both are glazed with a curry-flavored marmalade. Be sure the coals are low-glowing so the sugary glaze won't scorch.

    1 tablespoon butter or margarine
    ¼ cup finely chopped onion
    1 teaspoon curry powder
 1½ pounds lean ground lamb
    ⅓ cup fine dry bread crumbs
    2 eggs, slightly beaten
    ⅛ teaspoon pepper
    4 to 8 slices fresh or canned pineapple
      Marmalade glaze (recipe follows)

Melt butter in a wide frying pan over medium heat; add onion and curry powder and cook until onion is limp. Remove from heat and cool slightly. Thoroughly mix in lamb, bread crumbs, eggs, and pepper. With your hands, shape meat into compact balls the size of ping-pong balls.

Divide meat evenly and thread onto 4 to 6 sturdy metal skewers. Baste meat as well as pineapple slices with glaze; then arrange kebabs and pineapple on a lightly greased grill 4 to 6 inches above a solid bed of low-glowing coals. Cook, turning and basting frequently, until well browned on all sides (5 to 10 minutes). Makes 4 to 6 servings.

Marmalade glaze. In a pan, combine 1 cup **orange marmalade,** 2 teaspoons **curry powder,** and 2 tablespoons **water.** Heat, stirring, until well blended.

Grilled Lamb Logs in Tortillas

Open or covered grill • Cooking time: 10–15 minutes

You'll need only a few minutes to turn out these hearty barbecued sandwiches. Ground lamb, shaped into logs, is wrapped in bacon, then grilled and served in warm flour tortillas.

 1½ pounds lean ground lamb
    ⅓ cup finely chopped onion
    ¼ cup fine dry bread crumbs
    ¼ cup pine nuts or slivered almonds
    1 clove garlic, minced or pressed
    1 egg
    1 teaspoon salt
    ½ teaspoon dry rosemary
    ¼ teaspoon pepper
   12 slices bacon
    6 warmed flour tortillas (directions follow)

(Continued on next page)

In a bowl, combine lamb, onion, crumbs, nuts, garlic, egg, salt, rosemary, and pepper. Divide mixture into 6 equal portions and shape each into a log about 5 inches long.

In a frying pan over medium heat, partially cook bacon to remove excess fat; bacon should still be limp. Wind 2 slices of bacon around each log, securing ends with wooden picks. If made ahead, cover and chill for as long as 8 hours.

Place logs on a lightly greased grill 4 to 6 inches above a solid bed of medium-glowing coals. Turn as needed to brown all sides, and watch closely for flare-ups from bacon drippings. Cook for 10 to 15 minutes or until bacon is crisp and meat is no longer pink when slashed. Makes 6 servings.

Warmed flour tortillas. Stack 6 flour tortillas on a sheet of aluminum foil, sprinkling a few drops of water on each tortilla. Wrap tightly and place on grill over indirect heat (make sure package is not over any burning coals). Heat for 8 to 10 minutes, turning frequently.

Persian Lamb Bars

Open or covered grill • Cooking time: About 20 minutes

Offer this dish with hot, crusty white rice and grilled tomatoes. Both side dishes can finish on the barbecue while the meat cooks.

> 1½ **pounds lean ground lamb**
> 1 **large onion, finely chopped**
> 1 **egg, lightly beaten**
> 1 **teaspoon salt**
> ¼ **teaspoon pepper**
> 2 **tablespoons all-purpose flour**
> 3 **cups hot cooked rice**
> 3 or 4 **green onions and tops, thinly sliced**
> ½ **teaspoon garlic salt**
> 4 **tablespoons butter or margarine**
> 4 to 6 **small tomatoes, halved**
> **Butter or margarine**
> **Dry rosemary**
> **Salt and pepper**

In a bowl, mix together lamb, onion, egg, salt, pepper, and flour until well combined. Shape mixture into 4 to 6 patties, each about 5 inches long, 1½ inches wide, and 1 inch thick.

Combine rice, onion, and garlic salt. Melt the 4 tablespoons butter in a small frying pan; add rice mixture and press down lightly to form a round patty shape. Place pan on a grill 4 to 6 inches above a solid bed of glowing coals.

Lightly grease grill around pan and arrange lamb patties on grill. Cook meat, turning once, for about 10 minutes per side or until well browned. Do not stir rice.

After lamb and rice have cooked for 15 minutes, dot tomatoes with a little butter and sprinkle with rosemary, then with salt and pepper to taste. Place tomatoes, cut-side-up, along edge of grill (not directly over coals) to heat for remaining 5 minutes.

To serve, use a spatula to loosen rice in pan; then invert pan onto a serving platter so that bottom brown crust shows on top. Arrange patties and tomatoes around rice. Makes 4 to 6 servings.

Lemon Lamb Steaks

Open or covered grill • Cooking time: 12–15 minutes

Steaks cut from the broad end of a leg of lamb are delicious when grilled. These are lemon-flavored and simple, yet special.

> ⅔ **cup salad oil**
> ⅓ **cup lemon juice**
> 1 **medium-size onion, chopped**
> 1 **teaspoon** *each* **salt and oregano leaves**
> ¼ **teaspoon pepper**
> 4 **lamb steaks, each ¾ to 1 inch thick**
> **Lemon slices**
> **Parsley**

Combine oil, lemon juice, onion, salt, oregano, and pepper; pour over lamb. Cover and refrigerate for 4 hours or until next day.

Lift lamb from marinade and drain briefly (reserve marinade). Arrange on a lightly greased grill 4 to 6 inches above a solid bed of glowing coals. Cook, turning and basting occasionally with reserved marinade, for 12 to 15 minutes or until lamb is well browned on both sides but still pink in center when slashed. Garnish with parsley and lemon slices. Makes 4 servings.

Portuguese Shoulder Lamb Chops

Open or covered grill • Cooking time: 20–25 minutes

Shoulder lamb chops make excellent cuts for the grill. Marinate them first in one of these two tasty marinades made with red wine and oil.

> **Cumin-cinnamon marinade or Pickling**
> **spice marinade (recipes follow)**
> 5 or 6 **shoulder lamb chops, each ¾ inch**
> **thick**

Pour either of the marinades over chops; cover and refrigerate for at least 8 hours or until next day.

(Continued on page 56)

POCKETFUL of spicy lamb cubes, vegetables, and unflavored yogurt makes a whole-meal sandwich with Middle Eastern flair. (Lamb Sandwich Buffet recipe on page 52)

Remove chops from marinade and drain briefly (reserve marinade). Place on a lightly greased grill 4 to 6 inches above a solid bed of glowing coals. Cook, basting frequently with reserved marinade, for about 20 to 25 minutes or until meat is well browned on both sides but still pink in center when slashed. Makes 5 or 6 servings.

Cumin-cinnamon marinade. Combine 1 cup **dry red wine**, ½ cup **olive oil** or salad oil, 3 cloves **garlic** (minced or pressed), 1 teaspoon *each* **salt** and **ground cumin**, ¾ teaspoon **ground cinnamon**, ⅓ cup finely chopped **onion**, and 1 tablespoon **cumin seed**.

Pickling spice marinade. Combine 1 cup **dry red wine**, ¼ cup *each* **salad oil** and **wine vinegar**, 2 cloves **garlic** (minced or pressed), 1 teaspoon **salt**, ½ cup chopped **onion**, 1 tablespoon **whole mixed pickling spice**, 4 **whole cloves**, and ¼ teaspoon **ground cloves**.

Indian Lamb Chops

Open or covered grill • Cooking time: About 30 minutes

You add eight spices to the yogurt, and the result is a superbly seasoned mixture that comes originally from northern India. The spicy yogurt serves as the marinade, baste, and sauce.

> 2 **medium-size onions**
> 6 **sprigs fresh coriander (cilantro) and 1 tablespoon ground coriander (or substitute a total of 2 tablespoons ground coriander)**
> 2 **teaspoons ground cumin**
> 1½ **teaspoons *each* pepper, ground cloves, and ground cardamom**
> 1 **teaspoon *each* ground ginger, poppy seed, and ground cinnamon**
> 2½ **tablespoons melted butter or margarine**
> 2 **cups (1 pint) unflavored yogurt**
> 6 **tablespoons lemon juice**
> 12 **round-bone lamb chops, each 1 inch thick**

In a blender, place onion, coriander, cumin, pepper, cloves, cardamom, ginger, poppy seed, cinnamon, butter, yogurt, and lemon juice; whirl until smooth. Pour over chops; cover and refrigerate for 2 to 4 hours or until next day.

Lift chops from marinade and drain briefly (reserve marinade). Arrange on a lightly greased grill 4 to 6 inches above a solid bed of glowing coals. Cook, turning and basting occasionally, for about 15 minutes per side or until meat is well browned on both sides but still pink in center when slashed.

Warm reserved marinade in a pan on grill and serve as a sauce. Makes 12 servings.

Butterflied Lamb & Mushrooms

Open or covered grill • Cooking time: About 50 minutes

When it's butterflied—boned and spread out flat—a leg of lamb can be barbecued in less than an hour. Serve this lamb with grilled mushroom caps stuffed with a savory onion mixture.

> 1 **cup olive oil or salad oil**
> ⅔ **cup burgundy or other dry red wine**
> ¼ **teaspoon *each* thyme and oregano leaves**
> 1 **teaspoon salt**
> ¼ **teaspoon pepper**
> 1 **leg of lamb (5½ to 6½ lbs.), boned and butterflied**
> 8 **very large mushrooms, about 3 inches in diameter**
> 1½ **cups finely chopped onion**
> ¼ **cup butter or margarine**
> **Salt and pepper**

Combine oil, wine, thyme, oregano, salt, and pepper. Remove and reserve stems from mushrooms; place caps in a small bowl. Place lamb in a deep bowl and pour ¾ of marinade over lamb, ¼ over mushroom caps. Cover both and refrigerate for 2 to 4 hours.

Lift lamb from marinade and drain briefly (reserve marinade). Place on a lightly greased grill 4 to 6 inches above a solid bed of low-glowing coals. Cook, turning and basting frequently, for about 50 minutes or until meat is well browned but still pink in center when slashed.

As meat cooks, chop reserved mushroom stems and combine with onion. Melt butter in a frying pan, add onion mixture, and cook until tender (about 5 minutes). Add salt and pepper to taste.

After meat has cooked for 30 to 35 minutes, lift mushroom caps from marinade and drain briefly, hollow-side-down. Place caps hollow-side-down, on grill for 5 minutes. Turn over, fill with onion mixture, and grill for another 10 minutes. Makes about 8 servings.

Grilled Minted Lamb Shanks

Open or covered grill • Cooking time: About 30 minutes

You can precook the lamb shanks and marinate them a day in advance.

    4 to 6 pounds lamb shanks, cracked
        Water
    ¾ cup dry white wine
    2 tablespoons *each* lemon juice and
        chopped parsley
    2 cloves garlic, minced or pressed
    ⅓ cup honey
    1 teaspoon salt
    1½ teaspoons chopped fresh or dry mint

Place lamb shanks in enough water to cover; simmer, covered, until fork tender (about 45 minutes). Drain and let cool.

Combine wine, lemon juice, parsley, garlic, honey, salt, and mint. Place shanks in a deep bowl, pour marinade over shanks, cover, and refrigerate for at least 4 hours or until next day.

Lift shanks from marinade and drain briefly (reserve marinade). Place on a lightly greased grill 4 to 6 inches above a solid bed of low-glowing coals. Cook, turning and basting occasionally with reserved marinade, for about 30 minutes or until lamb is well browned and very tender when pierced. Makes 4 to 6 servings.

Garlic Lamb with Coffee Baste

Covered grill • Cooking time: About 2 hours

Strong coffee adds a rich flavor to this delicious baste. Don't use a very dark roasted type such as espresso — it could give a bitter flavor.

    1 bone-in leg of lamb (about 6 lbs.)
    4 or 5 cloves garlic, peeled and slivered
        Pepper
    ⅓ cup strong hot coffee and
    ⅓ cup melted butter or margarine
    1 teaspoon grated lemon peel

Using a small pointed knife, slit meat and insert garlic in several places. Rub lamb with pepper.

Bank about 20 low-glowing coals on each side of fire grill and place a metal drip pan in center. Place grill 4 to 6 inches above drip pan; grease grill lightly. Place lamb on grill directly above drip pan. Cover barbecue and adjust dampers according to manufacturer's directions.

Combine coffee, butter, and lemon peel. After meat has cooked for 30 minutes, baste occasionally with coffee mixture. Cook for about 1½ hours more or until meat thermometer inserted in thickest

portion (but not touching bone) registers 145° for rare, 155° for medium. Add 5 or 6 briquets on each side of fire every ½ hour to maintain a constant temperature. Makes about 8 servings.

Lime-flavored Leg of Lamb

Covered grill • Cooking time: About 2 hours

Here's an easily prepared basting sauce made with canned daiquiri mix and white wine, to add zest to a lamb roast.

    1 can (6 oz.) daiquiri mix
    ½ cup dry white wine
    2 tablespoons butter or margarine
    ½ teaspoon crushed dry rosemary
    1 bone-in leg of lamb (about 6 lbs.)

In a pan, combine daiquiri mix, wine, butter, and rosemary; heat until butter melts.

Bank about 20 low-glowing coals on each side of fire grill and place a metal drip pan in center. Place grill 4 to 6 inches above drip pan; grease grill lightly. Place lamb on grill directly above drip pan. Cover barbecue and adjust dampers according to manufacturer's directions.

Cook, basting occasionally, for about 2 hours or until meat thermometer inserted in thickest portion (but not touching bone) registers 145° for rare, 155° for medium. Add 5 or 6 briquets on each side of fire every ½ hour to maintain a constant temperature. Makes about 8 servings.

Split-bone Leg of Lamb

Covered grill • Cooking time: About 1 hour

Ask your butcher to do this: remove the tail bone and shank bone from a leg of lamb and, instead of removing the leg bone, saw it in two, lengthwise, splitting it right up the middle. The result is a butterflied piece of meat with an attractive curved bone along both outer edges.

    ⅓ cup olive oil or salad oil
    3 tablespoons lemon juice
    ½ teaspoon *each* instant minced onion and
        crushed dry rosemary
    ¼ teaspoon *each* sugar and coarsely
        ground pepper
    1 clove garlic, minced or pressed
    1 bone-in leg of lamb (about 6 lbs.), split
        lengthwise through center of leg bone

Combine oil, lemon juice, onion, rosemary, sugar, pepper, and garlic.

(Continued on page 59)

Bank about 20 medium-glowing coals on each side of fire grill and place a metal drip pan in center. Place grill 4 to 6 inches above drip pan; grease grill lightly. Place lamb, bone-side-down, on grill for 10 minutes to brown. Be sure it is directly over drip pan. Then turn lamb over, bone-side-up. Cover barbecue and adjust dampers according to manufacturer's directions.

Cook, basting occasionally, for 45 to 50 minutes longer or until meat is well browned on both sides but still pink in center when slashed. To serve, remove bones and slice meat across the grain in thin, slanting slices. Makes 6 to 8 servings.

Stuffed Shoulder of Lamb

Covered grill or spit-roasted • Cooking time: 2–2½ hours

A boned and rolled lamb shoulder encases a piquant fruit and herb mixture. *(Pictured on opposite page)*

> 2 packages (8 oz. *each*) mixed dried fruit, pitted and cut in pieces
> ½ cup chopped onion
> 1 teaspoon *each* grated lemon peel and dry rosemary
> ⅔ cup water
> 1 boned lamb shoulder (3 to 4 lbs.)
> Salt and pepper
> Regular-strength chicken broth
> 1 tablespoon cornstarch
> 2 tablespoons water

In a pan combine fruit, onion, lemon peel, rosemary, and the ⅔ cup water. Cook, uncovered, over medium heat, stirring often, until liquid is absorbed (about 6 minutes). Let cool.

Sprinkle inside of lamb with salt and pepper to taste. Spread ½ of fruit mixture over inside of roast. Roll roast and tie securely in many places (about 1 inch apart); tuck in ends and tie in several places around length of roll as well as width.

For covered grill cooking, bank about 20 low-glowing coals on each side of fire grill and place a metal drip pan in center. Place grill 4 to 6 inches above drip pan; grease grill lightly. Place meat on grill directly over drip pan. Cover barbecue and adjust dampers according to manufacturer's directions. Cook roast for about 2 hours or until meat thermometer inserted into thickest part of roast registers 145° for rare, 155° for medium. Add 5 or 6 briquets on each side of fire every ½ hour to maintain a constant temperature.

For spit-roasting, arrange enough low-glowing coals to form a solid rectangular bed about 6 inches

TUCKED INSIDE boneless lamb shoulder roast is delicious mixture of dried fruit and herbs (recipe above). Whole artichokes, potatoes, and carrots bake in foil alongside (recipes on page 89).

across and extending 3 to 4 inches beyond ends of the meat (see illustration, page 11). Coals should be about 2 inches behind an imaginary wall extending from spit to firebed. Place metal drip pan directly beneath and in front of spit. Place lamb on spit as directed in Basic Recipe: Spit-roasted Leg of Lamb, page 49. Cook for 2 to 2½ hours or until meat thermometer inserted in thickest portion (but not touching spit) registers 145° for rare, 155° for medium. Add 5 or 6 briquets to the fire every ½ hour, spacing them evenly, to maintain a constant temperature.

When roast is cooked, push coals aside and allow roast to stand (or continue to turn on spit) while you prepare gravy: Skim and discard fat from pan drippings. Measure drippings and add enough chicken broth to make 2 cups. Also add reserved fruit mixture. Blend cornstarch with water and stir into drippings. Cook, stirring, until thickened and boiling. Add salt and pepper to taste. As you carve roast, cut the long ties but leave the short ones intact. Makes 6 to 8 servings.

Barbecued Boned Lamb

Open or covered grill • Cooking time: 40–50 minutes

A butterflied leg of lamb can be cut into three separate roasts — two thick pieces (top round and sirloin tip) and one thinner piece (bottom round). When you barbecue them all at once, put the top round and sirloin tip on first; then add the bottom round about 10 minutes later. Each roast cooks to prefection despite the difference in size.

> ¼ cup lemon juice
> 1 large clove garlic, minced or pressed
> ½ teaspoon *each* crushed dry rosemary, thyme leaves, and prepared mustard
> 1 leg of lamb (about 6 lbs.), boned, butterflied, and divided into sections

Combine lemon juice, garlic, rosemary, thyme, and mustard. Pour over lamb pieces and rub evenly into meat. Cover and chill for at least 4 hours or until next day.

Lift lamb from marinade and drain briefly. Place top round and sirloin tip (2 thickest pieces) on lightly greased grill 4 to 6 inches above a solid bed of medium-glowing coals. Cook for about 10 minutes, then turn. Place bottom round with attached shank meat on grill and cook, turning each piece as needed to brown evenly, until all the meat is done to your liking. For medium-well, allow a total of about 50 minutes for top round and sirloin tip, 40 minutes for bottom round (cut a slash to test — meat should still be slightly pink inside). Makes 6 to 8 servings.

POULTRY

Poultry cooked over coals takes on a gloriously rich brown color, yet remains succulent and flavorful inside its crisp coat. Availability and versatility make chicken the most popular bird for the barbecue. It can be cooked whole, in halves or quarters, or by the piece. It adapts to any number of marinades as easily as to butter-basting. Not least, it can be grilled, spit-roasted, or smoked under cover. Adventurous cooks who wish to branch out will find they can prepare game hens, turkeys, ducks—even wild birds— with no more fuss than a chicken demands.

Basic Recipe: Chicken Parts on a Grill

Open or covered grill • Cooking time: 30–50 minutes

If you barbecue on an open grill, the best way to cook chicken is to cut it in pieces, quarters, or halves. These lie fairly flat and cook by direct heat from the coals.

> 1 broiler-fryer chicken (3 to 3½ lbs.), cut in
>   pieces, quarters, or halves
> Salt to taste
> Marinade or baste (optional)

Rinse chicken and pat dry. For quarters and halves, hook wing tips back behind body joint, akimbo-style. If you wish, marinate chicken (see Favorite Poultry Marinades & Bastes, page 62). To retain juices, salt *after* cooking.

Brush chicken with a baste; or, if marinated, lift chicken from marinade and drain briefly (reserve marinade). Arrange chicken, skin-side-up, on a lightly greased grill 4 to 6 inches above a solid bed of low-glowing coals.

Cook, turning and basting occasionally with baste or reserved marinade, for 40 to 50 minutes for leg pieces, quarters, or halves; for about 30 minutes for breast pieces. Chicken is done when meat near bone is no longer pink when slashed. Makes 4 servings.

Basic Recipe: Whole Chicken on a Covered Grill

Covered grill • Cooking time: About 1 hour

Here's a foolproof method for barbecuing whole chickens. Since the cover converts the barbecue into an oven, the chicken slowly cooks over indirect heat until it's golden brown all over.

> 1 whole broiler-fryer chicken (3 to 3½ lbs.)
> Salt to taste
> Marinade or baste (optional)

Remove giblets and reserve for other uses; rinse chicken and pat dry. Hook wing tips back behind body joint, akimbo-style. Marinate (see Favorite Poultry Marinades & Bastes, page 62) or stuff bird, if you wish, with your favorite stuffing. To retain juices, salt *after* cooking.

Bank about 20 low-glowing coals on each side of fire grill and place a metal drip pan in center. Place grill 4 to 6 inches above drip pan; grease grill lightly.

Drain bird, if marinated, and insert a meat thermometer into fleshy part of thigh but not touching bone. Place chicken, breast-side-up, on grill directly over drip pan. Cover barbecue and adjust dampers according to manufacturer's directions.

Cook for about 30 minutes, then baste. Continue basting every 10 minutes until chicken is done (about 60 minutes total or when meat thermometer registers 180° to 185°). Joints should move easily, and juices should run clear when skin is pierced. Makes 4 servings.

Basic Recipe: Whole Turkey on a Covered Grill

Covered grill • Cooking time: 15 minutes per pound

Turkey, the holiday favorite, roasts brown and juicy—and with little attention—in a covered barbecue. Since turkey is fairly inexpensive, consider barbecuing a small turkey for family meals and informal gatherings. *(Pictured on page 74)*

> 1 hen turkey (8 to 15 lbs.) or 1 tom turkey
>   (16 to 25 lbs.)
> Turkey baste (recipe follows)

When buying a turkey, allow ¾ to 1 pound turkey per person—that will be ample for second helpings. If you buy a frozen bird, thaw it in one of the following ways:
• To defrost turkey in refrigerator, place bird on a tray and partially open or puncture plastic wrap. Store in refrigerator, allowing 2 to 4 days (or about 24 hours for each 6 pounds of turkey) for it to thaw.
• To thaw turkey at room temperature, place unopened plastic-wrapped turkey in a large paper bag and set aside. Allow about 1 hour thawing time per pound.
• To thaw turkey in a hurry, place unopened plastic-wrapped turkey in a pan of cool water; change water frequently. Allow about ½ hour thawing time per pound.

Remove neck and giblets and reserve for other uses; rinse turkey and pat dry. Prepare your favorite stuffing, allowing about ¾ cup stuffing per pound of turkey for birds that weigh up to 14 pounds. For larger birds (15 pounds or more), allow about ½ cup per pound.

Fill neck cavity of bird with stuffing; fasten neck skin back with a skewer. Lightly stuff body cavity; secure opening with skewers and lace closed with cord. Tie legs together and tie wings to body.

Bank 20 to 25 medium-glowing coals on each side of fire grill and place a metal drip pan in center. Place grill 4 to 6 inches above drip pan; grease grill lightly. Place bird in center of grill, breast-side-up, directly over drip pan. Cover barbecue and adjust dampers according to manufacturer's directions.

(Continued on next page)

Roast bird for about 15 minutes per pound or until meat thermometer inserted into fleshy portion of thigh (but not touching bone) registers 180° to 185°. Add 5 or 6 briquets to each side of fire every ½ hour to maintain a constant temperature. Brush bird frequently with baste during the last 1½ hours of cooking.

Turkey baste. Combine ¼ cup melted **butter** or margarine, ½ cup **dry sherry** or apple juice, and ½ teaspoon *each* dry **rosemary, paprika,** and **rubbed sage.**

Basic Recipe: Spit-roasted Chicken & Other Birds

Spit-roasted • Cooking time: 80–90 minutes

A spit slowly turns the bird — chicken, turkey, duck, or other fowl — for even cooking, but it also makes it partially self-basting, since any leftover baste rolls over the surface of the bird instead of dripping off immediately.

    1 whole broiler-fryer (3 to 3½ lbs.)
      Salt to taste
      Marinade or baste (optional)

Select a broiler-fryer chicken with a breadth of about 4 to 4½ inches. Rinse and pat dry; remove giblets and reserve for other uses. If you wish, marinate bird (see Favorite Poultry Marinades and Bastes, at right). To retain juices, salt *after* cooking.

Drain bird, if marinated, and run spit through *exact center* of bird — bird's weight must be evenly distributed around the spit or it will drag against the motor. Set spit forks in breast and thigh and tighten them with your fingers. Then pick up spit at both ends and turn it. If one side drags downward, place bird a little more toward the light side or add a balance weight pointed toward the light side. A very slight tendency to spin doesn't matter, as the motor can overcome it. Tie wings and legs securely to body. When bird is balanced, tighten forks with pliers to be sure forks do not loosen during cooking.

Arrange enough glowing coals to form a solid rectangular bed about 6 inches across and extending 3 to 4 inches beyond ends of the chicken (see illustration, page 11). Coals should be about 2 inches behind an imaginary wall extending from spit to firebed. Place metal drip pan directly beneath and in front of spit. Surface of chicken should be about 5 inches above surface of coals.

Position spit on barbecue and start motor. As bird cooks, baste frequently. Add 5 or 6 briquets evenly spaced every ½ hour to maintain a constant temperature.

As bird begins to develop a rich brown color, begin testing it for doneness. Protecting hands with paper towels, press thick part of thigh; when thigh meat is soft, bird is ready to serve. The total cooking time for a broiler-fryer chicken is 80 to 90 minutes or until meat thermometer inserted in fleshy part of thigh (but not touching bone or spit) registers 180° to 185°.

When bird is done, push coals away and let spit turn without heat for about 3 to 5 minutes before carving. Makes 4 servings.

Turkey. Follow instructions for spit-roasting a broiler-fryer chicken, with the following exceptions: select a turkey weighing no more than 12 to 14 pounds, with a breadth of about 7½ to 8 inches; cook for 4¼ to 4¾ hours or until meat thermometer inserted into thigh (but not touching bone or spit) registers 180° to 185°.

Game hens. Follow instructions for spit-roasting a broiler-fryer chicken, with the following exceptions: select game hens weighing 1¼ to 1½ pounds, with a breadth of about 3 to 3¼ inches; cook for 70 to 80 minutes.

Squab. Follow instructions for spit-roasting a broiler-fryer chicken, with the following exceptions: select a squab weighing ¾ to 1 pound, with a breadth of 2¾ to 3 inches; cook 50 to 60 minutes.

Domestic duck. Follow instructions for spit-roasting a broiler-fryer chicken, with the following exceptions: select a duckling weighing 4 to 5 pounds, with a breadth of 4 to 4½ inches; as duckling cooks, prick surface with fork to help release fat under skin; cook for 1¼ to 1¾ hours.

Favorite Poultry Marinades & Bastes

Here's a quartet of the marinades and bastes we like most — little sauces that add zest to all kinds of birds. For a brief discussion of the difference between a baste and a marinade, see page 14.

Basic Wine Marinade

Using a blender, combine 2 large, coarsely chopped **onions,** 3 cloves **garlic,** 1 teaspoon **pepper,** ⅛ teaspoon **cayenne,** ½ cup **white wine vinegar,** 1 cup **dry white wine,** ¼ cup **salad oil,** 1½ teaspoons crushed **thyme leaves,** ½ teaspoon grated **lemon peel,** 2 tablespoons **lemon juice,** and 1 teaspoon **honey.** Whirl until smooth. Marinate poultry for about 2 hours, then baste as it cooks.

(Continued on page 64)

NO FORKS ARE NEEDED at this barbecue when you serve chili-glazed chicken parts (recipe on page 64) with Dutch-oven peas that you eat with your fingers (recipe on page 88).

Ginger-Soy Marinade

Combine 2 tablespoons **salad oil,** ⅓ cup **soy sauce,** 2 tablespoons **honey** or firmly packed brown sugar, 1 tablespoon **red wine vinegar,** 1 teaspoon grated **fresh ginger root,** and 1 clove **garlic** (minced or pressed). Marinate poultry for 4 to 8 hours, then baste as it cooks.

Herb Butter Baste

Combine 6 tablespoons melted **butter** or margarine, 1 clove **garlic** (minced or pressed), ¾ teaspoon **pepper,** ½ teaspoon *each* **thyme, sage, oregano,** and **marjoram** leaves, and ½ teaspoon dry **basil.** Use as a baste on any poultry.

Green Onion Butter Baste

Beat together 1 cup soft **butter** or margarine, 3 tablespoons *each* finely chopped **parsley** and minced **green onion,** ¾ teaspoon *each* **dry mustard** and **fines herbes,** ¼ teaspoon **garlic powder,** ⅛ teaspoon **liquid hot pepper seasoning,** and a dash of **pepper.** Use as a baste on any poultry.

Lemon-basted Chicken with Peaches

Open or covered grill • Cooking time: 40–50 minutes

Chicken and fresh peaches from the grill make a colorful combination. As soon as you peel the fruit, brush it with lemon baste to prevent darkening. Grill peaches just long enough to heat throughout. To turn fruit, use two large spoons.

- ⅓ **cup lemon juice**
- 2 **tablespoons honey**
- 2 **broiler-fryer chickens (3 to 3½ lbs. *each*), halved**
- 6 **tablespoons melted butter or margarine**
- 4 **large freestone peaches or nectarines Additional honey (optional)**

Combine lemon juice and honey. Pour over chicken; turn quarters to coat all sides. Cover and refrigerate for about 1 hour.

Lift chicken from marinade and drain briefly (reserve marinade). Add butter to marinade, brush on chicken, and arrange, skin-side-up, on a lightly greased grill 4 to 6 inches above a solid bed of low-glowing coals. Cook, turning and basting frequently with reserved marinade, for 40 to 50 minutes or until meat near bone is no longer pink when slashed.

About 20 minutes before chicken is done, peel, halve, and pit peaches. Brush immediately with lemon baste. About 10 minutes before chicken is

done, place fruit halves, flat side down, on grill. Heat for 3 to 4 minutes, then turn, baste, and heat for 5 minutes more or until hot. If desired, drizzle a little honey over fruit just before serving. Makes 4 very generous servings; or snip each half in two with poultry shears for 8 smaller servings.

Chili-glazed Chicken

Open or covered grill • Cooking time: 40–50 minutes

Try serving this colorful, red-glazed chicken with steamed garden peas still in their pods. Our photograph on page 63 shows how peas in a Dutch oven cook right alongside the chili-glazed chicken.

- ⅓ **cup melted butter or margarine**
- 2 **cloves garlic, minced or pressed**
- 1 **teaspoon chili powder**
- ¼ **teaspoon *each* ground cumin and grated lime peel**
- 2 **tablespoons lime juice**
- 1 **broiler-fryer chicken (3 to 3½ lbs.), cut in pieces**

Combine butter, garlic, chili powder, cumin, lime peel, and lime juice; generously brush over chicken.

Arrange chicken, skin-side-up, on a lightly greased grill 4 to 6 inches above a solid bed of low-glowing coals. Cook, turning and basting frequently, for 40 to 50 minutes or until meat near bone is no longer pink when slashed. Makes 4 servings.

Savory Herb Chicken

Open or covered grill • Cooking time: 40–50 minutes

Sherry and soy sauce blend with herbs to give this marinade a mild teriyaki taste.

- 1 **cup dry sherry**
- ½ **cup salad oil**
- 1 **large onion, finely chopped**
- 1 **tablespoon Worcestershire**
- 1 **teaspoon *each* soy sauce, lemon juice, garlic powder, thyme leaves, oregano leaves, marjoram leaves, and dry rosemary**
- 2 **broiler-fryer chickens (3 to 3½ lbs. *each*), quartered**

Combine sherry, oil, onion, Worcestershire, soy, lemon juice, garlic powder, thyme, oregano, marjoram, and rosemary. Pour over chicken; turn quarters to coat all sides. Cover and refrigerate for at least 1 hour or until next day.

Lift chicken from marinade and drain briefly (reserve marinade). Arrange chicken, skin-side-up, on a lightly greased grill 4 to 6 inches above a solid bed of low-glowing coals. Cook, turning and basting occasionally with reserved marinade, for 40 to 50 minutes or until meat near bone is no longer pink when slashed. Makes 8 servings.

Ranch-style Chicken for a Hungry Dozen

Open or covered grill • Cooking time: 40–50 minutes

If possible, make the basting sauce at least 24 hours in advance to blend the flavors completely. A hint of hot pepper gives this chicken its character.

- ½ **cup white cider vinegar**
- ⅓ **cup salad oil**
- 1½ **teaspoons Worcestershire**
- ½ **teaspoon instant minced onion**
- 1 **clove garlic, minced or pressed**
- 1 **teaspoon paprika**
- 1½ **teaspoons catsup or tomato paste**
- 6 to 8 **drops liquid hot pepper seasoning**
- ¼ **teaspoon dry mustard**
- 3 **broiler-fryer chickens (3 to 3½ lbs. *each*), cut in pieces.**

Combine vinegar, oil, Worcestershire, onion, garlic, paprika, catsup, hot pepper seasoning, and dry mustard. Dip chicken pieces to coat; drain briefly (reserve baste).

Arrange chicken, skin-side-up, on a lightly greased grill 4 to 6 inches above a solid bed of low-glowing coals. Cook, turning and basting frequently, for 40 to 50 minutes or until meat near bone is no longer pink when slashed. Makes 10 to 12 servings.

Ginger Chicken Quarters

Open or covered grill • Cooking time: 40–50 minutes

A ginger-flavored sauce marinates and bastes the chicken. Toasted sesame seed combined with thickened leftover marinade makes a tasty sauce to spoon over the cooked chicken and rice.

- ⅓ **cup soy sauce**
- 1 **cup water**
- 1 **clove garlic, minced or pressed**
- 1 **tablespoon sugar**
- 2 **tablespoons dry sherry or lemon juice**
- 3 **tablespoons grated fresh ginger root or 1 teaspoon ground ginger**
- 1 **broiler-fryer chicken (3 to 3½ lbs.), quartered**
- ¼ **cup sesame seed**
- 2 **teaspoons *each* cornstarch and water Hot cooked rice**

Combine soy, water, garlic, sugar, sherry, and ginger. Pour over chicken; turn quarters to coat all sides. Cover and refrigerate for at least 4 hours or until next day, turning frequently.

Lift chicken from marinade and drain briefly (reserve marinade). Arrange chicken, skin-side-up, on a lightly greased grill 4 to 6 inches above a solid bed of low-glowing coals. Cook, turning and basting frequently with ⅓ cup of reserved marinade, for 40 to 50 minutes or until meat near bone is no longer pink when slashed.

Toast sesame seed in a frying pan over medium heat, stirring until golden. Pour in remaining 1 cup marinade. Blend cornstarch and water, stir into pan, and cook, stirring, until thickened. Spoon over chicken and rice. Makes 4 servings.

Rosemary Chicken Quarters

Open or covered grill • Cooking time: 40–50 minutes

An herb marinade, punctuated by rosemary, flavors these chicken quarters.

- ½ **cup olive oil or salad oil**
- 2 **teaspoons dry rosemary**
- 1 **teaspoon minced parsley**
- 2 **cloves garlic, minced or pressed**
- 2 **tablespoons lemon juice**
- ⅛ **teaspoon pepper**
- 1 **broiler-fryer chicken (3 to 3½ lbs.), quartered**

Combine oil, rosemary, parsley, garlic, lemon juice, and pepper. Pour over chicken; turn quarters to

coat all sides. Cover and refrigerate for at least 3 hours or until next day, turning occasionally.

Lift chicken from marinade and drain briefly (reserve marinade). Arrange chicken, skin-side-up, on a lightly greased grill 4 to 6 inches above a solid bed of low-glowing coals. Cook, turning and basting with reserved marinade, for 40 to 50 minutes or until meat near bone is no longer pink when slashed. Makes 4 servings.

Teriyaki Chicken Legs with Onions & Potatoes

Open or covered grill • Cooking time: 40–50 minutes

Ginger, honey, and soy sauce flavor this chicken as well as the potatoes and onions that cook alongside it on the grill.

⅔ cup soy sauce
⅓ cup honey
2 teaspoons grated fresh ginger root or
   ¾ teaspoon ground ginger
3 tablespoons dry sherry
½ cup salad oil
1 clove garlic, minced or pressed
½ cup thinly sliced green onion
6 chicken legs and thighs (about 3 lbs.),
   attached
¼ cup butter or margarine
2 large onions, thinly sliced
4 large, unpeeled new potatoes, cooked
   and thinly sliced

Combine soy, honey, ginger, sherry, oil, garlic, and green onion. Pour over chicken; turn pieces to coat all sides. Cover and refrigerate for at least 4 hours or until next day, turning frequently.

Lift chicken from marinade and drain briefly (reserve marinade). Arrange chicken on a lightly greased grill 4 to 6 inches above a solid bed of low-glowing coals. Cook, turning and basting frequently with reserved marinade, for 40 to 50 minutes or until meat near bone is no longer pink when slashed.

As soon as chicken is arranged on grill, set a frying pan beside it. Melt butter in pan, add onion, and cook, uncovered, stirring occasionally, for 20 minutes. Add potato slices and cook for about 15 minutes longer or until potatoes are hot throughout and onion is soft. Before serving, stir 2 to 4 tablespoons of marinade into potato and onion mixture. Makes 6 servings.

BARBECUED CHICKEN HALVES with brandied fruit are transformed into a festive entrée when warmed brandy is ignited, ladled over all before serving. (Recipe on page 68)

Chicken Legs with Garlic Baste

Open or covered grill • Cooking time: 40–50 minutes

Garlic is the primary flavor here, with subtle overtones from the hops in the beer.

½ cup (¼ lb.) butter or margarine
4 cloves garlic, minced or pressed
¼ cup chopped onion
1 cup beer
1 tablespoon minced parsley
½ teaspoon coarsely ground pepper
6 chicken legs and thighs (about 3 lbs.),
   attached, or 3 whole chicken breasts
   (about 3 lbs.), split

Melt butter in a small pan; add garlic and onion and cook over medium heat for about 5 minutes or until soft but not browned. Add beer and, stirring constantly, bring to a boil; then remove from heat. Add parsley and pepper. Roll chicken pieces in baste to coat thoroughly, then drain briefly; reserve baste.

Arrange chicken on a lightly greased grill 4 to 6 inches above a solid bed of low-glowing coals. Cook, turning and basting frequently with reserved garlic baste, for 40 to 50 minutes for legs and thighs (about 30 minutes for breasts) or until meat near bone is no longer pink when slashed. Makes 6 servings.

Chicken Provençal

Open or covered grill • Cooking time: 40–50 minutes

Mustard, garlic, and herbs coat chicken legs and thighs. When grilled, they develop a crisp skin over moist and succulent meat.

2 tablespoons Dijon mustard
2 teaspoons dry white wine or lemon juice
1 teaspoon Italian herb seasoning or ¼
   teaspoon *each* dry basil, dry rosemary,
   oregano leaves, and thyme leaves
1 teaspoon instant minced onion
1 clove garlic, minced or pressed
6 chicken legs and thighs (about 3 lbs.),
   attached

Combine mustard, wine, herb seasoning, onion, and garlic; stir until smooth. Spread mixture evenly over all sides of chicken pieces. Cover lightly and refrigerate for 2 to 4 hours.

Arrange chicken on a lightly greased grill 4 to 6 inches above a solid bed of low-glowing coals. Cook, turning frequently, for 40 to 50 minutes or until meat near bone is no longer pink when slashed. Makes 6 servings.

Chicken with Brandy Baste

Covered grill • Cooking time: 40–50 minutes

Two perfect partners — chicken and fruit — are basted with brandy and cooked together in a covered barbecue. *(Pictured on page 66)*

    2 broiler-fryer chickens (3 to 3½ lbs. *each*),
        halved
      Salt and pepper
    ½ cup (¼ lb.) melted butter or margarine
    ¼ cup *each* lemon juice, brandy, and firmly
        packed brown sugar
    1 cup pitted dark sweet cherries or canned
        pitted sweet cherries, drained
    6 apricots, halved and pitted, or canned
        apricot halves, drained
    2 tablespoons brandy (optional)

Sprinkle chicken with salt and pepper. Combine butter, lemon juice, the ¼ cup brandy, and sugar; turn chicken in baste to coat thoroughly; then drain briefly.

Arrange chicken, skin-side-up, on a lightly greased grill 4 to 6 inches above a solid bed of low-glowing coals. Cover barbecue, adjust dampers, and cook, turning and basting occasionally, for 40 to 50 minutes or until meat near bone is no longer pink when slashed.

After chicken has cooked for about 35 minutes, arrange cherries and apricots (cut-side-up) in 2 separate shallow metal pans. Brush fruit with basting sauce, then heat on grill beside chicken for the last 5 to 10 minutes.

To serve, place chicken on a platter, arrange apricots around it, and pour cherries over chicken. (Or heat cherries to bubbling, carefully pour the 2 tablespoons brandy over top, ignite, and spoon over chicken.) Makes 4 servings.

Spanish-style Chicken & Rice

Open or covered grill • Cooking time: 40–50 minutes

In this simple adaptation of Spanish *arroz con pollo,* you serve barbecued chicken quarters on a bed of colorful, spicy rice.

    ½ cup (¼ lb.) melted butter or margarine
    1 clove garlic, minced or pressed
    ¾ teaspoon savory leaves
    ½ teaspoon paprika
    ¼ teaspoon *each* ground cinnamon and
        tarragon
    1 broiler-fryer chicken (3 to 3½ lbs.),
        quartered
      Chorizo rice (recipe follows)

Combine butter, garlic, savory, paprika, cinnamon, and tarragon. Turn chicken in butter mixture to coat thoroughly; then drain briefly.

Arrange chicken, skin-side-up, on a lightly greased grill 4 to 6 inches above a solid bed of low-glowing coals. Cook, turning and basting frequently with butter mixture, for 40 to 50 minutes or until meat near bone is no longer pink when slashed. Reserve remaining butter mixture for chorizo rice.

Serve each chicken quarter over a mound of rice. Makes 4 servings.

Chorizo rice. Cut 2 **chorizo sausages** (2½ to 3 oz. *each*) into ½-inch slices. In a wide frying pan over medium heat, brown chorizo on all sides. Add 2 medium-size **onions** (finely chopped) and cook until soft and golden. Stir in 3 cups cooked **rice**, 1 cup frozen **peas** (thawed), and 1 **tomato** (peeled and coarsely chopped). Cover and cook over low heat, stirring once or twice, until hot (about 10 minutes); blend in remaining butter mixture.

Tumbled Chicken & Ribs

Spit-roasted • Cooking time: About 1½ hours

You'll need a cylindrical spit basket that attaches to your spit for this chicken and rib combination. Use a basket from 14 to 17 inches long and fill it not more than ¾ full.

    3 pounds country-style pork spareribs,
        thick-cut and meaty
   12 chicken thighs (about 3 lbs.)
      Salt and pepper

With a sharp knife, remove as much fat as possible from ribs and separate into individual blades. Center spit basket on spit rod and layer-fill with chicken and ribs. Do not overfill—⅔ to ¾ of basket is best, as meat must have room to tumble.

(Continued on next page)

Arrange enough low-glowing coals to form a solid rectangular bed about 6 inches across and extending 3 to 4 inches beyond ends of basket (see illustration, page 11). Coals should be about 2 inches behind an imaginary wall extending from spit to firebed. Place spit on barbecue 4 to 6 inches above firebed and start motor. Cook for about 1½ hours or until meat near bone is no longer pink when slashed. Add 5 or 6 briquets every ½ hour, spacing them evenly to maintain a constant temperature. After removing chicken and ribs from basket, season to taste with salt and pepper. Makes 8 to 10 servings.

Onion-stuffed Whole Chicken

Covered grill • Cooking time: About 1 hour

Canned onions offer a delicious surprise stuffing for this barbecued whole chicken.

  1 **large whole broiler-fryer chicken (3½ to 4 lbs.)**
  1 **clove garlic, halved**
  1 **can (1 lb.) small whole onions, drained**
  2 **bay leaves**
  ¼ **cup melted butter or margarine**
  ½ **teaspoon pepper**
  ¼ **teaspoon** *each* **thyme, oregano, and marjoram leaves**
  ¼ **teaspoon** *each* **dry basil and rubbed sage**
  2 **tablespoons dry sherry**

Remove giblets and reserve for other uses; rinse chicken and pat dry. Rub cut garlic over chicken skin, then put garlic in body cavity with onions and bay leaves. Combine butter, pepper, thyme, oregano, marjoram, basil, sage, and sherry; spoon 1 tablespoon of the mixture over onions in chicken cavity. Reserve remaining mixture for baste.

Close body cavity and secure with metal skewers; tie legs together. Also secure neck skin across opening with a skewer and tuck wing tips under, akimbo-style.

Bank about 20 low-glowing coals on each side of fire grill and place a metal drip pan in center. Place grill 4 to 6 inches above drip pan; grease grill lightly. Brush bird with baste and place, breast-side-down, on grill directly over drip pan. Cover barbecue, adjust dampers according to manufacturer's directions, and cook for 30 minutes. Turn chicken breast-side-up and cook, basting occasionally, for about 30 minutes longer or until meat thermometer inserted in thigh (but not touching bone) registers 185°.

Scoop out onions from chicken; discard bay leaves and garlic before offering onions with the meat. Makes 4 servings.

Spinach-stuffed Game Hens

Covered grill or spit-roasted • Cooking time: About 1 hour

Each game hen is stuffed with an herb-rice mixture accented with fresh spinach and water chestnuts. Heat any leftover stuffing and serve alongside. *(Pictured on page 71)*

  2 **game hens (1½ lbs.** *each***), thawed**
  Spinach rice stuffing (recipe follows)
  Green onion baste (recipe follows)

Remove giblets and reserve for other uses; rinse birds and pat dry. Prepare spinach rice stuffing; put ¾ to 1 cup stuffing in body cavity of each hen. Secure body openings with metal skewers and tie legs together. Also secure skin across neck openings with skewers and tuck wing tips under, akimbo-style. Prepare green onion baste.

For covered grill cooking, bank about 20 low-glowing coals on each side of fire grill and place a metal drip pan in center. Place grill 4 to 6 inches above drip pan; grease grill lightly. Arrange birds breast-side-up on grill, directly over drip pan. Cover barbecue and adjust dampers according to manufacturer's directions. Cook, basting occasionally, for 45 minutes to 1 hour or until thigh meat is soft when squeezed (protect hands).

For spit-roasting, arrange enough medium-glowing coals to form a solid rectangular bed about 6 inches across and extending 3 to 4 inches beyond ends of the meat (see illustration, page 11). Coals should be about 2 inches behind an imaginary wall extending from spit to firebed. Place metal drip pan directly beneath and in front of spit. Run spit through exact center of birds. Place spit on barbecue about 6 inches above firebed and start motor. Cook, basting birds frequently, for 70 to 80 minutes or until thigh meat is soft when squeezed.

Snip each bird in half with poultry shears, if desired. Makes 2 or 4 servings.

Spinach-rice stuffing. In a frying pan, heat 2 tablespoons **salad oil**. Add 1 bunch (about ¾ lb.) **spinach** (cut in ¼-inch strips), 1 can (7 oz.) **water chestnuts** (drained and sliced), and ½ cup *each* minced **green onion** and diced **celery**. Cook, stirring, for 1 minute or until spinach wilts; remove from heat. Add 2 cups cold cooked **rice**, ¼ teaspoon **dry rosemary**, **salt** and **pepper** to taste.

Green onion baste. Beat ½ cup soft **butter** or margarine until fluffy; blend in 1½ tablespoons *each* finely chopped **parsley** and finely minced **green onion**, ½ teaspoon *each* **dry mustard** and **fines herbes**, ¼ teaspoon **garlic powder**, ⅛ teaspoon *each* **salt** and **liquid hot pepper seasoning**, and a dash of freshly ground **pepper**.

Buttery Game Hens

Covered grill • Cooking time: 45–60 minutes

An herb butter and a glistening apricot glaze flavor these delicious birds. One whole bird makes a very generous serving — snip birds in half with poultry shears for regular servings.

    4 game hens (about 1¼ lbs. *each*), thawed
      Herb butter (recipe follows)
    2 tablespoons lemon juice
    ¼ cup strained apricot jam, warmed
      Watercress sprigs and fresh or canned
        apricot halves for garnish

Remove giblets and reserve for other uses. Prepare herb butter and place 1 tablespoon in body cavity of each hen. Secure body and neck openings with wooden picks and tie legs together. Tuck wing tips under, akimbo-style. In a pan, melt remaining herb butter with lemon juice.

Bank about 20 low-glowing coals on each side of fire grill and place a metal drip pan in center. Place grill 4 to 6 inches above drip pan; grease grill lightly. Place birds, breast-side-up, on grill directly over drip pan. Cover barbecue and adjust dampers according to manufacturer's directions.

Cook, basting occasionally with butter-lemon mixture, for 45 minutes to 1 hour or until thigh meat is soft when squeezed (protect hands with paper towels). During the last 10 to 15 minutes, brush birds with jam; continue cooking until nicely glazed. Remove birds to a warm platter, snip birds in half with poultry shears, if desired, and garnish with watercress and apricot halves. Makes 4 to 8 servings.

Herb butter. Combine ½ cup (¼ lb.) soft **butter** or margarine, 2 tablespoons chopped **chives**, and ½ teaspoon **dry rosemary.**

Turkey Parts with Barbecued Yams

Covered grill • Cooking time: About 90 minutes

Yams wrapped in foil cook alongside turkey legs, wings, thighs — all good choices for barbecuing.

    6 turkey legs, wings, or thighs (or a
        combination of parts)
    6 medium-size yams
      Butter or margarine, softened
      Jelly baste (recipe follows)
      Yam condiments (suggestions follow)

Arrange turkey parts on a lightly greased grill 4 to 6 inches above a solid bed of low-glowing coals.

Wash yams, pat dry, rub with butter, pierce skin, and wrap in foil; place on grill beside turkey. Cover barbecue and adjust dampers according to manufacturer's directions.

Cook for about 15 minutes or until turkey skin just becomes golden. Turn turkey pieces over, cover, and continue cooking, turning pieces frequently to brown well on all sides, for 65 to 75 minutes longer or until meat near bone is no longer pink when slashed. During last 20 minutes, brush turkey parts frequently with jelly baste. Meanwhile, turn yams occasionally. Every ½ hour add 5 or 6 briquets to fire, spacing them evenly, to maintain a constant temperature.

Remove turkey and yams to serving platter. Offer condiments for yams. Makes 6 servings.

Jelly baste. In a pan combine ½ cup **red currant jelly,** ¼ cup *each* **port** and **catsup,** 2 tablespoons **butter** or margarine, and ½ teaspoon **Worcestershire.** Heat until bubbling.

Yam condiments. Offer in separate containers ½ cup **butter** or margarine; and ½ cup firmly packed **brown sugar;** and ½ cup chopped **roasted salted peanuts** mixed with ½ cup shredded **coconut.**

Duckling with Orange Baste

Covered grill • Cooking time: About 2 hours

In a covered barbecue, duckling roasts to a delicate golden brown when basted with this orange-honey combination.

    1 whole duckling (4½ to 5 lbs.), thawed
    ½ cup orange juice
    ¼ cup soy sauce
    1 teaspoon honey
    ⅛ teaspoon pepper

Remove giblets and reserve for other uses; rinse duckling and pat dry. Secure neck skin to back with skewer. Pierce duck skin well with fork. Truss duckling so that wings and legs are held firmly against body.

In a pan, combine orange juice, soy, honey, and pepper; heat until well blended.

Bank about 20 glowing coals on each side of fire grill and place a deep metal drip pan in center. Place grill 4 to 6 inches above drip pan; grease grill lightly. Place duckling, breast-side-up, on grill directly above drip pan. Cover barbecue and adjust

(Continued on page 75)

SPIT-ROASTED GAME HENS are stuffed with herb-rice mixture featuring fresh spinach and water chestnuts (recipe on page 69). Sautéed tomatoes (recipe on page 90) make savory complement.

Game Birds

When the successful hunter comes home, he or she may have a dozen or more birds in tow. While many will probably be tucked away in the family freezer, some will undoubtedly find their way to the table at once. Either way, pluck and clean the birds as soon as possible after the "shoot." Plucking is usually preferred to skinning because the skin adds much to the flavor and appearance.

Birds should be hung or aged before cooking. In some cases, as in pheasant, for example, aging makes a tremendous difference in the tenderness of the meat. "Hanging" a bird simply means letting it age, well wrapped, at room temperature for 2 days or in the refrigerator for 4 days. If you freeze the birds, do the "hanging" after they have thawed.

Basic Recipe: Whole Wild Duck

Open or covered grill • Cooking time: 15–25 minutes

Wild duck is not usually stuffed; however, a slice of onion, a rib of celery, or a piece of apple may be put into the cavity for flavoring. More adventuresome cooks might try 2 or 3 juniper berries or springs of parsley instead.

> **2 ducks (2 to 3½ lbs. *each*), cleaned and hung**
> **Slice of vegetable or fruit suggested above (optional)**
> **Melted butter or margarine**
> **Brandy (optional)**
> **Salt and pepper**

Carefully wipe ducks inside and out with a damp cloth. Place slice of vegetable or fruit in cavity for flavoring, if desired. Skewer cavity closed.

Bank about 20 glowing coals on each side of fire grill and place a metal drip pan in center. Place cooking grill 4 to 6 inches above drip pan; grease grill lightly.

Place ducks, breast-side-up, on well-greased grill directly over drip pan. Cover barbecue and adjust dampers according to manufacturer's directions. (Make a hood of foil to enclose ducks if cooking on an open grill.)

Cook for about 10 minutes, then baste with melted butter. Continue basting every 5 minutes until ducks are done to your liking when slashed. (Ducks on the rare side will be juicer, and more tender and flavorful.)

If crisp skin is desired, pour a little heated brandy over each duck when it is done; ignite brandy and allow to flame. Salt and pepper to taste. Makes 4 servings.

Wild Duck Paprika

Covered grill • Cooking time: 25–35 minutes

A simple combination of butter, Worcestershire, and paprika flavors these crisp-skinned birds. An aluminum foil boat encases each duckling, ensuring even cooking throughout.

> **4 ducks (1 to 2½ lbs. *each*), cleaned and hung**
> **About ½ cup (¼ lb.) butter or margarine, at room temperature**
> **Worcestershire**
> **Paprika**

Carefully wipe ducks inside and out with a damp cloth. Lightly rub butter over entire skin of each duck. Place on individual sheets of heavy-duty foil and mold into boatlike casings, extending foil up sides of each duck just to breast.

Pour 3 or 4 squirts of Worcestershire over each duck; then sprinkle enough paprika to completely coat breast (ducks should look red all over).

Bank about 20 glowing *(very hot)* coals on each side of fire grill; set cooking grill 4 to 6 inches above coals. Place foil-wrapped ducks together in a shallow metal pan; set pan on grill in center so that no portion is directly over coals. Cover barbecue and adjust dampers to manufacturer's directions (vents should be open to ensure hottest fire). Cook for about 25 minutes, then check for doneness. Depending upon how hot you can keep the fire, or the weight of the birds, and on the way you like them, ducks will be done in 25 to 35 minutes.

To serve, peel off foil wrapping. Offer 1 whole duck to each person for 4 servings or split in half with poultry shears for 8 servings.

Grilled Duck Halves

Open or covered grill • Cooking time: 15–25 minutes

Split down the back and then pressed out flat, these ducks may be cooked either in a hinged wire broiler or directly on the grill. A light, orange butter baste enhances the duck's natural flavor.

- 2 mallard ducks (1½ to 3 lbs. *each*), cleaned and hung
- ½ cup (¼ lb.) melted butter or margarine
- 2 teaspoons *each* dry mustard and grated lemon peel
- 4 teaspoons grated orange peel

Carefully wipe ducks inside and out with a damp cloth. Split down the backbone with poultry shears; set aside.

Combine melted butter, mustard, and lemon and orange peels; mix sauce thoroughly. Lightly baste both sides of duck with sauce (reserve remaining sauce). Place in a hinged wire broiler and close securely (or place on lightly greased grill); place 4 to 6 inches above a solid bed of medium-glowing coals. Cook, turning and basting often with reserved sauce, for 7 to 10 minutes on each side or until done to your liking.

Divide each duck again at breast bone into 2 portions and serve. Makes 2 to 4 servings.

Pheasant with Cashew Stuffing

Spit-roasted • Cooking time: 50–60 minutes

Whole pheasant spit-roasts to a rich, golden brown enclosing a light, nutty stuffing of cashews and bacon. If the pheasant was frozen and not hung beforehand, you can do this after thawing—it will make a big difference in the meat's tenderness.

- 1 young pheasant (2½ to 3 lbs.), cleaned and hung
- 1 cup coarsely chopped cashew nuts
- 1 cup regular-strength chicken broth
- 4 strips bacon, cooked and crumbled
- 2 tablespoons butter or margarine
- ½ teaspoon salt
  Dash of pepper
- 3 strips bacon

Carefully wipe pheasant inside and out with a damp cloth; set aside.

In a small pan over low heat, simmer cashews in chicken broth until tender and liquid is absorbed. Mix in crumbled bacon, butter, salt, and pepper. Lightly stuff bird with cashew mixture and close with skewers. Tie wings to body or tuck in back akimbo-style. Tie legs together. Wrap 3 strips of bacon over breast of pheasant and secure with wooden picks.

Arrange enough medium-glowing coals to form a solid rectangular bed about 6 inches across and extending 3 to 4 inches beyond ends of bird (see illustration, page 11). Coals should be about 2 inches behind an imaginary wall extending from spit to firebed. Place metal drip pan directly beneath and in front of spit. Surface of pheasant should be about 6 inches above surface of coals.

Run spit through exact center of bird; set spit forks in breast and thigh and test for balance (see Basic Recipe: Spit-roasted Chicken & Other Birds, page 62). Position spit on barbecue and start motor. Every ½ hour add 5 or 6 briquets to fire, spacing them evenly, to maintain a constant temperature.

Protecting hands with paper towels, press thick part of thigh; pheasant is cooked when thigh meat is soft (50 to 60 minutes). Makes 2 servings.

dampers according to manufacturer's directions. Cook, basting occasionally, for 1¾ to 2 hours or until thigh meat is soft when squeezed (protect hands with paper towels). Add 5 or 6 briquets to each side of fire every ½ hour to maintain a constant temperature. Makes 4 servings.

Peking-style Duck

Covered grill • Cooking time: 2–2¼ hours

There's a whole ritual involved in eating Peking-style duck. Each guest slices morsels of crisp skin and succulent meat, then prepares a kind of sandwich in a flour tortilla with Chinese hoisin sauce (available in Oriental markets), coriander, and green onion.

2 ducklings (4½ to 5 lbs. *each*), thawed
1 teaspoon *each* ground ginger and cinnamon
½ teaspoon ground nutmeg
¼ teaspoon *each* ground cloves and pepper
¼ cup soy sauce
  About 1 cup canned hoisin sauce
1 to 1½ dozen flour tortillas
  About 1½ cups slivered green onion, including some tops
½ to 1 cup coarsely chopped fresh coriander (cilantro)

Remove giblets and reserve for other uses. With fork, pierce duck skin well. Trim off excess neck skin; fasten remaining skin to back with skewer.

Blend ginger, cinnamon, nutmeg, cloves, and pepper. Dust about ½ teaspoon of the spice mixture inside each duck, then rub remaining mixture evenly over exterior of birds. Leave body cavity open for more even cooking.

Bank about 20 glowing coals on each side of firebed and place a deep metal drip pan in center. Arrange birds, breast-side-up, on a well-greased grill 4 to 6 inches above drip pan. Cover barbecue, leaving dampers open to maintain a hot fire. Add 5 or 6 briquets to each side of fire every ½ hour to maintain a constant temperature.

Combine soy and 2 tablespoons of the hoisin sauce. Cook ducks for about 2 to 2¼ hours or until thigh meat is soft when squeezed (protect hands with paper towels). During last 20 minutes of cooking, brush ducks frequently with soy mixture.

Meanwhile, lightly dampen tortillas, cut in halves or quarters, stack, and wrap in foil. Heat in a 350° oven for 10 to 15 minutes or until steamy; place in a napkin-lined basket to keep warm. Put remaining hoisin sauce, green onion, and coriander in separate serving bowls.

To eat, spread tortilla pieces with hoisin; slice small pieces of duck skin and meat (trimming out fat) and put on tortilla. Top with a few green onion slivers and some coriander, and fold to eat out of hand. Makes 6 to 8 servings.

Boned Duck Halves

Covered grill • Cooking time: 2–2¼ hours

You halve and partially bone the uncooked duck. To serve, snip each boned half in two, making four individual servings.

4½ to 5-pound duckling, thawed
⅓ cup lemon juice
1 clove garlic, minced or pressed
¼ teaspoon *each* dry mustard and rosemary
⅛ teaspoon pepper
2 tablespoons honey

Remove giblets and reserve for other uses. To halve and partially bone duck, place duck breast-side-up and cut along breastbone with tip of knife. Continue cutting meat free from breastbone following contour of rib cage and cutting through joint where wing is connected. Continue along side of duck toward thigh joint, then twist and pull gently until thighbone is free from socket. Continue until one half of duck is removed from carcass. Repeat on other side of duck to make 2 semiboneless halves—wing and leg bones remain. (Save rib cage and backbone for soup stock if you wish.) Trim off excess skin. Pierce duck skin well with fork and place duck halves, skin-side-up, in a shallow pan.

Combine lemon juice, garlic, mustard, rosemary, and pepper. Pour over duck, cover, and refrigerate for 2 to 4 hours.

Bank about 20 glowing coals on each side of firebed and place a deep metal drip pan in center. Lift duck from marinade and drain briefly (reserve marinade). Arrange halves, skin-side-up, on a well-greased grill 4 to 6 inches above drip pan. Cover barbecue, leaving dampers open to maintain a hot fire. Add 5 or 6 briquets on each side every ½ hour to maintain a constant temperature.

Stir honey into reserved marinade. Cook duck for 2 to 2¼ hours or until thigh meat is soft when squeezed (protect hands with paper towels). During the last 30 minutes of cooking, brush duck with honey mixture. To serve, snip halves in two with poultry shears. Makes 4 servings.

WITH LITTLE ATTENTION, even the biggest turkey roasts to oven-brown perfection in covered kettle barbecue. You'll be amazed at how succulent meat remains.
(Recipe on page 61)

SEAFOOD

The roster of outstanding fish for the barbecue focuses
on those with pronounced flavors—salmon, trout,
albacore, mackerel, rockfish, sablefish, sturgeon, swordfish,
and striped bass. This is because smoke from the fire
should enhance, not overpower, the taste of the fish itself.
Cut in fillets or steaks, or left whole, these
flavorful fish can be marinated in herbaceous or spicy sauces,
or just butter-basted and still emerge with individual
character. Shrimp, clams, and other shellfish cook
properly with just a few minutes
on the grill. Sheltered
by their shells,
they retain fresh-
caught flavors—a quality
that makes them especially
suitable for beach-
fire barbecuing.

Basic Recipe: Fish Steaks & Fillets

Open or covered grill • Cooking time: 15–20 minutes

All fish steaks and fillets need frequent basting while barbecuing to prevent drying out. If you plan to cook fish directly on the grill, pieces should be at least ¾ inch thick. For thinner pieces you will need a hinged wire basket or broiler (see illustration, page 6) for easier turning.

6 fish steaks or fillets (about ½ pound
***each*), cut 1 inch thick**
Marinade or baste

Wipe fish with damp cloth. If you prepare a marinade (see Favorite Seafood Marinades & Bastes, at right), place fish in a large plastic bag in a rimmed baking pan and pour in marinade. Twist-tie bag closed, refrigerate, and marinate for 1 to 2 hours.

Lift fish from marinade and drain briefly (reserve marinade). Arrange fish on well-greased grill 4 to 6 inches above a solid bed of low-glowing coals. Cook, turning once and basting frequently with reserved marinade or other baste, for 15 to 20 minutes or until fish flakes readily when prodded in thickest portion with a fork. Makes 6 servings.

Basic Recipe: Large Whole Fish

Open or covered grill • Cooking time: 30–60 minutes

Large whole fish — salmon, bass, or one of the larger fresh-water varieties — are delicious when barbecued, but because of their size and weight, they require special handling. Our recipe can be used for any large whole fish weighing 3 to 8 pounds. To calculate the number of servings a fish will yield, figure about ½ pound of fish per person.

1 whole fish (3 to 8 pounds), cleaned,
scaled, and head removed (if desired)
Salt and pepper
1 lemon, sliced
1 onion, sliced
Parsley sprigs

Wipe fish with damp cloth, inside body cavity and outside. Sprinkle with salt and pepper inside cavity; tuck in lemon and onion slices and several sprigs of parsley. Cut a piece of heavy-duty foil which, when doubled, fits exactly against one side of fish from head to tail to provide two layers of protection and support. Fold foil and press smoothly to fish. If desired, insert a meat thermometer into thickest portion of fish (but not touching dorsal fin).

Bank about 20 glowing coals on each side of fire grill; place grill 4 to 6 inches above coals. Place fish, foil-side-down, on grill directly over space between coals. Arrange a wad of foil under tail to support it and protect it slightly from heat.

Cover barbecue and adjust dampers according to manufacturer's directions. (If cooking on an open grill, tear off enough heavy-duty foil to cover grill *completely;* tuck foil over edges of barbecue to seal in heat and smoke.)

Allow 10 minutes cooking time per 1-inch thickness of fish, measured in thickest portion. At the end of that time (30 minutes for a 3-inch-thick fish, for example), lift cover or foil and test for doneness. Thermometer should register 120° and fish should flake readily when prodded in thickest portion with a fork.

When fish is done, hold a warm serving platter close to grill; slide a wide metal spatula carefully under foil-lined fish and ease onto platter. Lift off top layer of skin, if desired. Cut down directly to backbone, slide a wide spatula between flesh and ribs, and lift off each serving. When top half has been served, lift and remove backbone (sever from head, if necessary) and cut down to skin to serve remaining half (be careful not to catch foil lining).

Favorite Seafood Marinades & Bastes

The following flavorful marinades and bastes may be used on fish fillets, steaks, or small whole fish. Each recipe makes enough for 2 to 3 pounds of fish.

Seafood Teriyaki Marinade
Combine ½ cup **soy sauce,** 1 tablespoon **sugar,** 2 teaspoons *each* **lemon juice** and minced **fresh ginger** (or ½ teaspoon ground ginger), 1 clove **garlic** (minced or pressed), and 2 tablespoons **dry sherry** or sake. Pour over fish; cover and refrigerate for 30 minutes to 2 hours, turning fish occasionally.

Easy Fish Marinade
Combine ¼ cup *each* **salad oil** and **dry sherry,** 2 tablespoons **soy sauce,** 1 teaspoon *each* **Worcestershire** and **garlic powder,** and ⅛ teaspoon **pepper.** Pour over fish; cover and refrigerate for 30 minutes to 2 hours, turning fish occasionally.

Seafood Herb-Wine Marinade
In a small pan, combine 1 cup **dry white wine,** ¼ cup **lemon juice,** 2 tablespoons **white wine vinegar,** 2 cloves **garlic** (minced or pressed), 1 teaspoon **tarragon leaves** or dry rosemary, and 2 tablespoons melted **butter** or margarine (or use

salad oil). Heat to simmering, remove from heat, cover, and let stand for 1 hour. Pour over fish; cover and refrigerate for 30 to 60 minutes.

Orange-Soy Marinade

Combine ½ cup *each* **soy sauce** and **orange juice,** ¼ cup *each* **catsup** and finely chopped **parsley,** 2 cloves **garlic** (minced or pressed), 2 tablespoons **lemon juice,** and ¼ teaspoon **pepper.** Pour over fish; cover and refrigerate for 30 to 60 minutes.

Italian-style Marinade

Combine ¾ cup **olive oil** or salad oil, ¼ cup **white wine vinegar,** 1 clove **garlic** (minced or pressed), and ½ teaspoon **oregano leaves.** Pour over fish; cover and refrigerate for 30 minutes to 2 hours.

Seafood Butter Baste

Combine ¼ cup melted **butter** or margarine and ¼ cup **lemon juice,** dry sherry, or dry vermouth. If you wish, add ¼ teaspoon *each* **dry rosemary** and **thyme leaves,** or ½ teaspoon tarragon leaves. Use to baste fish frequently during cooking.

Lemon-Onion Baste

Combine ½ cup **lemon juice,** ¼ cup **salad oil,** ¼ teaspoon *each* **salt** and **sugar,** dash of **pepper,** and ⅛ cup chopped **green onion.** Use to baste fish frequently during cooking.

Savory Salmon Steaks

Open or covered grill • Cooking time: About 20 minutes

Bottled salad dressing is a seasoning short cut for these richly flavored salmon steaks.

 4 **salmon steaks** (*each* about ½ lb. and about ¾ inch thick)
 Salt and pepper
 ¼ cup **bottled Italian-style salad dressing** or hickory-flavored dressing
 ½ teaspoon **paprika**
 1 teaspoon **minced or grated onion**
 2 teaspoons **lemon juice**
 Parsley for garnish

Wipe fish with damp cloth. Sprinkle both sides of salmon lightly with salt and pepper. Combine salad dressing, paprika, onion, and lemon juice. Pour over steaks, coating both sides, and let stand for about 20 minutes.

Lift steaks from marinade and drain briefly (reserve marinade). Place on heavy-duty foil and turn up edges to form a shallow pan. Place pan on barbecue grill 4 to 6 inches above a solid bed of glowing coals. Cover barbecue and adjust dampers according to manufacturer's directions. (Make

a hood of foil to enclose fish if cooking on an open grill.) Cook, basting frequently with reserved marinade, for about 20 minutes or until fish flakes readily when prodded in thickest portion with a fork. Makes 4 servings.

Tomato-Orange Sea Bass

Open or covered grill • Cooking time: 15–20 minutes

The tart-sweet taste of the tomato sauce that covers these bass comes from orange juice and peel.

 2 tablespoons olive oil or salad oil
 1 medium-size onion, finely chopped
 2 cloves garlic, minced or pressed
 1 can (1 lb.) tomatoes
 1½ teaspoons chili powder
 ½ teaspoon *each* salt and dry basil
 ⅛ teaspoon ground cumin
 4 large sea bass steaks, *each* about 1 inch thick
 Salt and pepper
 1 large juicy orange
 1½ teaspoons cornstarch
 Chopped parsley

Heat oil in a frying pan over medium heat; add onion and garlic and cook until soft but not browned. Stir in tomatoes and their liquid (break up tomatoes with a spoon), chili powder, salt, basil, and cumin. Simmer tomato sauce, uncovered, stirring occasionally, for 25 to 30 minutes or until sauce is thick and reduced to about 1¾ cups.

Wipe fish with damp cloth; sprinkle lightly with salt and pepper. Place on heavy-duty foil and turn up edges to form a shallow pan.

Using a vegetable peeler, cut thin strips from outer peel of orange. Cut strips into slivers to make 1 teaspoon slivered peel; set aside. Squeeze juice from orange and measure out ⅓ cup (reserve remaining juice for other uses); blend juice into tomato sauce. Spread sauce evenly over fish.

Place fish in its foil pan on grill 4 to 6 inches above a solid bed of medium-glowing coals. Cook for 15 to 20 minutes or until fish flakes readily when prodded in thickest portion with a fork. Transfer fish to a warm serving platter.

Pour liquid from foil pan into a heat-resistant pan and place on grill. Blend a little of the liquid into cornstarch, then blend cornstarch mixture into remaining pan liquid. Cook, stirring, until thickened; pour over fish. Sprinkle with reserved orange peel and parsley. Makes 4 servings.

BAY LEAVES FLAVOR whole fish enclosed in grape leaves and filled with thin slices of onion and lemon. (Recipe on page 83)

Albacore with Lemon Butter

Open or covered grill • Cooking time: 10–20 minutes

Barbecued albacore is basted with a delicious lemon concoction. Bacon strips hold the soft flesh together until it is cooked and firm.

> 6 albacore steaks (*each* about ½ pound and all about the same thickness), skin removed
> 6 strips bacon
> ½ cup (¼ lb.) butter or margarine
> 1 clove garlic, minced or pressed
> ¼ cup lemon juice
> 2 tablespoons chopped parsley
> Salt and pepper

Wipe fish with damp cloth. Remove bone and dark-colored meat from steaks with a sharp knife; push steaks back into shape with fingers. Wrap a strip of bacon around circumference of each and secure with a wooden pick. In a small pan, melt butter and add garlic, lemon juice, and parsley; set aside.

Place steaks on well-greased grill 4 to 6 inches above a solid bed of low-glowing coals. Cook, turning once and basting frequently with lemon butter, until fish is browned and flakes readily when prodded with a fork. For a 1-inch-thick piece of fish, measured in thickest portion, allow 10 minutes. Transfer to a warm serving platter; sprinkle with salt and pepper to taste. Makes 6 servings.

Swordfish with Mushrooms

Open or covered grill • Cooking time: 10–15 minutes

Try the lemony sautéed-mushroom topping with other fish, too — it also complements halibut, snapper, and lingcod.

> 2 pounds swordfish steaks, *each* about 1 inch thick
> 3 tablespoons lemon juice
> ¼ cup dry white wine or water
> 1 clove garlic, minced or pressed
> ½ teaspoon *each* oregano leaves, salt, and pepper
> ¼ teaspoon fennel seed, crushed
> ½ pound mushrooms, sliced
> 2 tablespoons olive oil or salad oil
> 2 or 3 green onions, thinly sliced

Wipe fish with damp cloth and cut into serving-size pieces. Combine lemon juice, wine, garlic, oregano, salt, pepper, and fennel. Place fish in a plastic bag, pour in marinade, and twist-tie bag closed. Chill for 1 to 2 hours, turning bag often.

Lift fish from marinade and drain briefly (reserve marinade). Place on a well-greased grill 4 to 6 inches above a solid bed of medium-glowing coals. Cook, turning once, for 5 to 8 minutes on each side or until fish flakes readily when prodded in thickest portion with a fork.

As soon as fish goes on the grill, sauté mushrooms in oil until limp (about 5 minutes). If you use a heavy metal frying pan, you can cook mushrooms on grill over the coals. Stir in reserved marinade and simmer for about 2 minutes.

Transfer cooked fish to a serving plate; top with mushroom sauce and sprinkle with green onion. Makes about 4 servings.

Sablefish Teriyaki

Open or covered grill • Cooking time: About 15 minutes

Sablefish, often labeled "butterfish" or "black cod," has a buttery tenderness and mild flavor that is enhanced when the fish is cooked on the barbecue.

> 2 to 3-pound piece of sablefish, cut lengthwise into 2 fillets
> ¼ cup soy sauce
> ½ cup dry sherry or apple juice
> 2 tablespoons lemon juice
> ½ teaspoon grated fresh ginger or ¼ teaspoon ground ginger

Wipe fish with a damp cloth. Cut two pieces of heavy-duty foil the size of the fillets and place against skin sides of fish; crimp edges. In a pan, combine soy, sherry, lemon juice, and ginger; simmer for 2 to 3 minutes or until thickened slightly. Brush soy mixture on flesh sides of fish; let stand for about 30 minutes.

Place fish, foil-side-down, on grill 4 to 6 inches above a solid bed of medium-glowing coals. Cover barbecue and adjust dampers according to manufacturer's directions. (Make a hood of foil to enclose fish if cooking on an open grill.) Cook, basting several times with soy mixture, for about 15 minutes or until fish flakes readily when prodded in thickest portion with a fork. Makes 4 to 6 servings.

Parmesan Mackerel

Open or covered grill • Cooking time: About 10 minutes

A crusty cheese coating and smoky flavor complement the taste of mackerel. Have the fish boned when you purchase it at the market.

    4 whole mackerel (*each* about 1¼ lbs.),
        cleaned and scaled; or 2 mackerel
        (*each* about 2½ lbs.), boned and filleted
    ½ cup *each* salad oil and lemon juice
    2 tablespoons chopped parsley
    1 teaspoon dry basil
    1 cup grated Parmesan cheese
    ½ teaspoon garlic salt

Wipe fish with damp cloth. If using fillets, cut them into pieces about 4 inches long. Combine oil, lemon juice, parsley, and basil. Pour over fish; cover and chill for 1 hour, turning once or twice.

Lift fish from marinade and drain briefly (reserve marinade). On a piece of wax paper or in a shallow pan, combine cheese and garlic salt. Thickly coat fish in cheese mixture; pat lightly. Arrange in single layer on wax paper until ready to grill.

Drizzle fish with reserved marinade and place on a well-greased grill 4 to 6 inches above a solid bed of medium-glowing coals. Cook, turning once and drizzling often with reserved marinade, until fish is browned and flakes readily when prodded in thickest portion with a fork. For a 1-inch-thick piece of fish (measured in thickest portion), allow 10 minutes. (Allow same ratio of thickness to time —1 inch: 10 minutes—for fish of all thicknesses.) Makes 4 to 6 servings.

Company Fish & Vegetables

Open grill • Cooking time: 15–20 minutes

You can prepare the lemon-herb dressing and begin to marinate the fish the night before or early on the day of serving. You can also cook the vegetables until barely tender, then finish cooking them on the grill.

    6 firm-textured fish steaks (such as
        salmon, lingcod, sea bass, sturgeon, or
        halibut), *each* 1 inch thick
    Lemon-herb dressing (recipe follows)
    6 to 8 small whole red-skinned new
        potatoes, cooked
    About 4 medium-size zucchini, cut into
        2-inch pieces and cooked
    ½ cup melted butter or margarine
    ¼ cup *each* grated Parmesan cheese and
        finely chopped parsley
    Lemon wedges

Wipe fish with damp cloth and arrange in a shallow pan. Pour over lemon-herb dressing; cover and refrigerate for at least 6 hours or until next day, turning once.

Thread potatoes and zucchini on separate skewers and brush generously with melted butter. Arrange vegetables on one side and fish on the other side of a well-greased grill 4 to 6 inches above a solid bed of low-glowing coals. Cook vegetables, turning frequently, until browned on all sides. Cook fish, basting frequently with butter and turning once with a spatula, until it flakes readily when prodded in thickest portion with a fork (about 8 to 10 minutes per side).

As soon as vegetables are done, transfer to a shallow casserole; toss with all but 1 tablespoon of the remaining butter, as well as cheese and parsley. Transfer fish to a serving platter; drizzle with remaining 1 tablespoon butter and garnish with lemon wedges. Makes 6 servings.

Lemon-herb dressing. Combine ⅓ cup **lemon juice**; ⅓ cup *each* **olive oil** and **salad oil** (or use ⅔ cup salad oil); 1 teaspoon *each* **sugar, salt, dry mustard**; 1 teaspoon **Italian herb seasoning** (or ¼ teaspoon *each* dry rosemary, oregano leaves, and dry basil); ¼ teaspoon **pepper**; 1 clove **garlic** (minced or pressed); and 1 tablespoon **instant minced onion.** Shake or stir to blend. Makes 1 cup.

Butterflied Trout with Nut Butter

Open or covered grill • Cooking time: About 10 minutes

Boned and butterflied trout marinates in an Italian-flavored dressing before being grilled.

    4 whole trout (*each* about ½ lb.), cleaned
        and scaled
    1½ cups bottled Italian-style dressing
    4 tablespoons butter or margarine
    ½ cup chopped salted macadamia nuts

To bone cleaned trout and keep head and tail in place, open body cavity; insert a sharp knife at head end under backbone and cut between ribs and flesh, releasing bones from fish back. (Take care not to cut through back of fish.) Repeat process to free other side. Ease backbone free, leaving back flesh of trout intact. Using kitchen scissors, snip backbone at head and tail; lift out bony skeleton and discard. Cut off and discard fins. Fish is now ready to be butterflied—spread out flat. Wipe with damp cloth.

Place butterflied trout in a shallow pan and pour over dressing; cover and let stand for about 30 minutes. Remove from marinade and drain briefly (reserve marinade). Place skin-side-down on well-greased grill 4 to 6 inches above a solid bed of low-glowing coals. Cook, brushing occasionally with reserved marinade, for about 10 minutes or until fish flakes readily when prodded in thickest portion with a fork. Meanwhile, melt butter in a heavy metal pan on grill and add nuts; keep warm to serve over cooked fish. Makes 4 servings.

Bacon-wrapped Stuffed Porgy

Open or covered grill • Cooking time: 10 minutes

Crisp bits of celery and onion are tucked into these small whole fish, and bacon wraps the outside.

  4 whole porgies (*each* 10 to 12 oz.), cleaned
    and scaled
  ½ cup *each* finely chopped onion and celery
  ¼ cup chopped parsley
  1 teaspoon dry chervil
  ½ teaspoon salt
  ¼ teaspoon pepper
  4 to 8 strips bacon
  1 lemon, thinly sliced

Wipe each fish with damp cloth, inside cavity and outside. Combine onion, celery, parsley, chervil, salt, and pepper; mix well. Divide stuffing evenly into 4 parts and tuck 1 part into cavity of each fish. Wrap 1 or 2 bacon slices crosswise around each fish and secure with wooden picks.

Place fish on well-greased grill 4 to 6 inches above a solid bed of low-glowing coals. Cook, turning once, until well browned and fish flakes readily when prodded in thickest portion with a fork. For a 1-inch-thick fish (measured in thickest portion), allow 10 minutes.

Transfer fish to a warm serving platter. Arrange lemon slices on fish and serve immediately. Makes 4 servings.

Barbecued Butterflied Salmon

Open or covered grill • Cooking time: 45–60 minutes

Lightly smoked, slowly cooked salmon is butterflied first for easier handling. A pungently flavored soy-butter sauce is served alongside.

  6 to 8-pound salmon, head, tail and back
    fin removed
  3 tablespoons melted butter or margarine
    Soy-butter sauce (recipe follows)

Butterfly fish from the stomach side, then bone it, leaving skin intact. Trim any white membrane from inside belly area of fish. Wipe fish with damp cloth, inside body cavity and outside. Lay salmon out, skin-side-down, on heavy-duty foil; cut foil to follow outline of fish. Crimp edges of foil.

FISH IS DONE when it "flakes"–slides into natural divisions–when prodded gently in thickest part with fork.

Place on grill 4 to 6 inches above a solid bed of low-glowing coals. Brush fish with melted butter. Cover barbecue and adjust dampers according to manufacturer's directions. (If cooking on an open grill, tear off enough heavy-duty foil to cover grill *completely;* tuck foil over edges of barbecue to seal in heat and smoke.)

Cook for about 45 minutes; then start checking for doneness every 10 minutes. Salmon should flake readily when prodded in thickest portion with a fork. Add 5 or 6 briquets after 30 minutes, if necessary, to maintain a constant temperature.

Supporting fish with foil, slip onto a large serving platter. Lift pieces of salmon from foil with a spatula (skin will adhere to foil). Accompany with soy-butter sauce, but add sparingly because it is pungently flavored. Makes 10 to 12 servings.

Soy-butter sauce. In a pan, melt ¾ cup **butter** or margarine. Stir in 2 cloves **garlic** (minced or pressed), 1½ tablespoons *each* **soy sauce** and **dry mustard,** ⅓ cup dry **sherry** or regular-strength chicken broth, and 3 tablespoons **catsup.** Keep warm on the grill with the salmon. Makes 1½ cups.

Onion-flavored Striped Bass

Open or covered grill • Cooking time: About 20 minutes

The firm, sweet flesh of striped bass grills well and is especially tasty when covered with an onion-laden barbecue sauce.

  1 whole striped bass (about 7 to 8 lbs.),
    dressed, skinned, and filleted; or 4 or 5
    striped bass fillets
  ½ cup salad oil
  ¾ cup *each* chopped onion and catsup
  ⅓ cup lemon juice
  3 tablespoons *each* sugar and
    Worcestershire
  2 tablespoons prepared mustard
  ½ teaspoon pepper
    Salt

Wipe fillets with damp cloth. Place a piece of heavy-duty foil (cut to fit) against the skin side of each fillet; press smoothly to fit; cover and chill.

In a pan, heat oil over medium heat; add onion and cook until soft. Add catsup, lemon juice, sugar, Worcestershire, mustard, pepper, and salt to taste. Simmer, uncovered, for 10 to 15 minutes or until thickened.

Place fish on grill, foil-side-down, 4 to 6 inches above a solid bed of medium-glowing coals. Cover barbecue and adjust dampers according to manufacturer's directions. (If cooking on an open grill, tear off enough heavy-duty foil to cover grill *completely;* tuck foil over edges of barbecue to seal in heat and smoke.) Cook, basting generously with onion mixture, until fish flakes readily when prodded in thickest portion with a fork. For a 2-inch-thick piece of fish (measured in thickest portion), allow 20 minutes. (Allow same ratio of thickness to time — 1 inch: 10 minutes — for fish of all thicknesses.) Serve with remaining onion mixture. Makes 8 to 10 servings.

Whole Salmon with Lemon Rice Stuffing

Open or covered grill • Cooking time: 30–60 minutes

This impressive whole salmon is lined with sliver-thin slices of grapefruit and stuffed with a lemony pilaf of mushrooms and rice.

> Lemon-rice stuffing (recipe follows)
> 1 whole cleaned salmon (4 to 8 lbs.)
> 1 small thin-skinned grapefruit
> Melted butter or margarine

Prepare lemon-rice stuffing (for a 4 to 5-lb. fish, use only half the recipe). Wipe fish with damp cloth, inside body cavity and out. Lightly pack stuffing into cavity; sew opening with heavy thread (wrap any leftover stuffing in foil and heat on grill).

Cut a piece of heavy-duty foil to fit one side of fish; grease foil generously. Slice grapefruit as thinly as possible; lay half the slices, overlapping slightly, on greased foil. Lay fish on grapefruit; then press foil smoothly to fit fish. Arrange remaining slices evenly on top of fish. If desired, insert a thermometer into thickest portion of fish (but not touching dorsal fin).

Bank about 20 medium-glowing coals on each side of fire grill; place grill 4 to 6 inches above coals. Place fish, foil-side-down, on grill directly over space between coals. Arrange a wad of foil under tail to support it and protect it slightly from heat. Drizzle fish with melted butter. Cover barbecue and adjust dampers according to manufacturer's direction. (If cooking on an open grill, tear off enough heavy-duty foil to cover grill *completely;* tuck foil over edges of barbecue to seal in heat and smoke.)

Cook, basting occasionally with melted butter, until fish flakes readily when prodded in thickest portion with a fork, or until meat thermometer registers 120°. For a 3-inch-thick fish (measure in thickest portion after stuffing), allow at least 30 minutes. (Allow same ratio of thickness to time—1 inch: 10 minutes — for fish of all thicknesses.)

To serve, see instructions for Basic Recipe: Large Whole Fish, page 77. Spoon out some stuffing to accompany each serving. A 4-pound salmon makes about 8 servings.

Lemon-rice stuffing. In a pan, melt 3 tablespoons **butter** or margarine. Add 1 cup sliced **celery** and 1 small **onion** (chopped); cook over medium-high heat until vegetables are soft (about 5 minutes). Add ¼ teaspoon **thyme leaves,** 2 teaspoons grated **lemon peel,** ¼ cup **lemon juice,** and 2½ cups **water.** Bring to a boil. Mix in 1¼ cups long-grain white **rice** and cover; reduce heat to low and cook for 20 minutes or until all liquid is absorbed.

Meanwhile, melt 3 tablespoons **butter** or margarine in a frying pan; add 1 to 2 cups sliced **mushrooms** and cook over medium heat until soft (about 5 minutes). When rice is done, stir in mushrooms, along with 1½ teaspoons **salt** and ⅛ teaspoon **pepper.** Makes enough for an 8-pound fish.

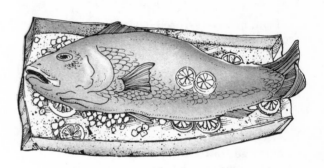

Fish with Bay Leaves

Open grill • Cooking time: 60 minutes

This method of barbecuing fish wrapped in grape leaves is similar to the one that was made popular in Provence, France. Try salmon, snapper, rock fish, striped bass, or sea trout. We used an 8-pound salmon and cooked it in a wire-hinged broiler (see page 6), but you can achieve the same effect by first wrapping the fish in grape leaves and then in a piece of soft chicken wire. (*Pictured on page 79*)

> 1 whole fish (3 to 10 lbs.), cleaned, scaled, and head removed (if desired)
> 5 to 10 slices *each* onion and lemon, cut about ½ inch thick
> Salt and pepper
> Fresh grape leaves
> 5 or 6 bay leaves

(Continued on next page)

Wipe fish with damp cloth, inside body cavity and outside. Lightly fill fish cavity with onion and lemon slices; sprinkle outside of fish with salt and pepper. Grease both sides of wire-hinged broiler; line bottom with grape leaves. Place fish in broiler on grape leaves, top with bay leaves and remaining grape leaves (fish and leaves will total 4 to 5 inches in thickest portion). Close broiler and secure tightly; sprinkle grape leaves with water.

Place fish on grill 4 to 6 inches above a sparse bed of glowing coals (scatter about 20 to 25 burning coals). Cook, turning broiler over every 15 minutes, for 50 to 60 minutes or until fish flakes readily when prodded in thickest portion with a fork (push grape leaves away with fork to test). Add 5 or 6 briquets after 30 minutes, if necessary, to maintain a constant temperature.

To serve, open broiler and peel off grape and bay leaves and skin from top of fish. Transfer fish to a warm serving platter. Cut down directly to backbone, sliding a wide metal spatula between flesh and ribs, and lift off each serving. Makes 6 to 20 servings.

Fish & Vegetable Kebabs

Skewer-cooked • Cooking time: 8–10 minutes

Any firm, meaty-textured fish such as salmon, albacore, lingcod, swordfish, or shark (sometimes sold as "thrasher") can be skewered with vegetables and quickly cooked on the barbecue. You'll either want to marinate the kebabs ahead of time or use a baste while they cook (see Favorite Seafood Marinades & Bastes, page 77).

    2 to 3 pounds fish (see suggestions above)
      Marinade or baste (optional)
    1 large onion, cut in 1-inch cubes
      Your choice of at least two of the
        following vegetables:
      2 medium-size green peppers, seeded and
        cut in 1-inch squares
      1 dozen tiny new potatoes (1 to 2 inches in
        diameter), cooked
      2 small zucchini, cut crosswise in
        1-inch-thick slices
      1 basket cherry tomatoes

Wipe fish with a damp cloth and cut into 1-inch cubes. Refrigerate until ready to use; or marinate, if desired.

If marinated, lift cubes and drain briefly (reserve marinade). Thread on skewers, alternating with vegetables. Place on well-greased grill 4 to 6 inches above a solid bed of low-glowing coals. Cook, turning occasionally and basting with reserved marinade or a baste, for 8 to 10 minutes or until fish flakes readily when prodded with a fork. Makes 4 to 6 servings.

Fish & Mushroom Skewers

Skewer-cooked • Cooking time: About 10 minutes

A lemon-oregano sauce is brushed over chunks of swordfish, whole mushrooms, and fresh bay leaves that have been threaded on skewers. Halibut or whole scallops may be substituted for the swordfish.

      Lemon-oregano sauce (recipe follows)
      About 16 whole bay leaves
      Hot water
    1¼ pounds swordfish or halibut steaks or 1
        pound scallops
      About 16 large mushrooms

Prepare lemon-oregano sauce. Soften bay leaves in enough hot water to cover for about 5 minutes; drain and set aside.

Wipe swordfish or halibut steaks with damp cloth and cut into 1¼-inch cubes (leaves scallops whole). Alternate fish pieces with bay leaves and mushrooms on 4 sturdy skewers. Brush each lightly with about 2 tablespoons lemon-oregano sauce.

Place skewers on well-greased grill 4 to 6 inches above a sparse bed of low-glowing coals (scatter about 15 to 20 burning coals). Cook, turning frequently, for about 10 minutes or until fish flakes readily when prodded with a fork. (Cook scallops just until opaque throughout, about 5 minutes.) Serve with remaining lemon sauce to spoon over individual servings. Makes 4 servings.

Lemon-oregano sauce. In a blender, combine ¼ cup fresh **lemon juice**, 1 clove **garlic** (minced or pressed), ¾ teaspoon **salt**, ¼ teaspoon **pepper**, and 1 **egg**. Whirl until lemon-colored and frothy. With blender set on lowest speed, add ¾ cup **olive oil** or salad oil, drop by drop at first, then in a thin stream, until sauce is thick and creamy. Stir in 1 tablespoon chopped fresh **oregano** or 1 teaspoon dry oregano leaves and 2 tablespoons minced **green onion.**

Spicy Marinated Shrimp

Skewer-cooked • Cooking time: About 8 minutes

Serve these flavorful shrimp on skewers as a hot hors d'oeuvre or over rice for a light supper entrée.

    4 tablespoons salad oil
    1 teaspoon salt
    ½ teaspoon *each* pepper and garlic powder
    6 tablespoons *each* chili sauce and vinegar
    2 tablespoons Worcestershire
    ⅛ teaspoon liquid hot pepper seasoning
    ½ cup lightly packed minced parsley
    2 pounds medium-size (30 to 32 per lb.) raw
        shrimp, shelled and deveined
    4 tablespoons melted butter or margarine

Combine oil, salt, pepper, garlic powder, chili sauce, vinegar, Worcestershire, hot pepper seasoning, and parsley. Pour over shrimp; cover and refrigerate for 1 to 2 hours.

Lift shrimp from marinade and drain briefly (reserve marinade). Thread onto skewers and place on a well-greased grill 4 to 6 inches above a solid bed of low-glowing coals. Cook, turning and basting with reserved marinade, for about 4 minutes on each side or until shrimp turn pink. Makes about 5 dozen appetizers or 6 to 8 entrée servings.

Mint-flavored Shrimp

Skewer-cooked • Cooking time: About 8 minutes

Mint-flavored shrimp, served right from the grill, make great appetizers.

    1 teaspoon chili powder
    1 tablespoon vinegar
    ¼ teaspoon pepper
    1 clove garlic, minced or pressed
    1 teaspoon *each* salt and dry basil
    1 tablespoon finely chopped fresh mint or
        crumbled dry mint
    ¾ cup salad oil
    2 pounds medium-size (30 to 32 per lb.) raw
        shrimp, shelled and deveined

In a bowl, stir together chili powder, vinegar, pepper, garlic, salt, basil, mint, and oil until well blended. Add shrimp, turning to coat. Cover and refrigerate for at least 4 hours or until next day.

Lift shrimp from marinade and drain briefly (reserve marinade). Thread onto skewers and place on a well-greased grill 4 to 6 inches above a solid bed of low-glowing coals. Cook, turning and basting frequently with reserved marinade, for about 4 minutes on each side or until shrimp turn pink. Makes about 5 dozen appetizers.

Quick Shellfish Picnic

Open grill • Cooking time: 6–8 minutes

Oysters, clams, and precooked hard-shell crab make a delicious combination for a spur-of-the-moment picnic at home or at the beach. For each person, include about 10 clams, 5 or 6 medium-size oysters, and ¼ of a large, cooked and cracked crab.

    40 clams
    20 to 24 medium-size oysters
    ½ cup (¼ lb.) butter or margarine, melted
    1 large hard-shell crab (about 2½ lbs.),
        cooked and cracked

Scrub clams and oysters in fresh water and arrange in a bowl. Place melted butter in a heat-resistant pan on outer edge of grill to keep warm.

Barbecue a few clams and oysters at a time, if you wish. Set any number of clams and oysters on the grill 4 to 6 inches above a solid bed of glowing coals. After about 3 minutes or when clams and oysters begin to open, turn them over and continue to cook until they pop wide open (about 3 to 4 more minutes). Protecting fingers with a napkin, hold clams and oysters over butter pan to drain juices into butter. Pluck out meat with fork, dip in butter, and eat. Serve cracked crab alongside to dip in butter. Makes 4 servings.

Easy Clambake for Six

Open grill • Cooking time: About 10 minutes

Pop-open clams dipped in flavored butter, and crusty, grill-cooked French bread combine in this do-it-yourself clambake for six.

    2 cups (1 lb.) butter or margarine, melted
    1 loaf (1 lb.) French bread, split lengthwise
    2 teaspoons garlic powder
    24 to 30 dozen large clams, well scrubbed in
        fresh water

Brush about ½ cup of the melted butter on bread halves; sprinkle with garlic powder and set aside.

Place clams on ungreased grill 4 to 6 inches above a solid bed of low-glowing coals. Place remaining butter in heat-resistant pan on edge of grill to warm. After 3 or 4 minutes or when clams begin to open, turn them over and continue cooking. Place French bread, cut-side-down, on grill to heat (about 5 minutes). Cut into pieces.

Clams will eventually pop wide open when done (about 4 or 5 more minutes). Protecting hands with a napkin, hold clams over butter pan and drain juices into butter. Pluck out clams with fork, and dip in butter to eat. Makes about 6 servings.

SIDE DISHES

Outdoor chefs quickly learn to take advantage of a good
fire. It is a simple matter to put a side dish on
the grill alongside the main course. Foil-wrapped or skewered
vegetables and casseroles add special flavors to any outdoor
meal. The side dishes may be prepared in advance in the kitchen,
then set to cook or reheat over low-glowing coals until
serving time. Breads—even desserts—heated over a
fire complement barbecued main dishes as well as add flavor
and variety to any outdoor meal.

Grilled French Bread

Open grill • Cooking time: About 5 minutes

Hot buttered French bread, with or without garlic, is a reliable standby for outdoor meals.

    ½ cup (¼ lb.) butter or margarine, at room
      temperature
    3 cloves garlic, minced or pressed
      (optional)
    1 loaf (1 lb.) French bread, split lengthwise

In a small pan over medium heat, melt butter; add garlic, if desired. Brush over bread halves. Place halves, cut-side-down, on grill 4 to 6 inches above a solid bed of low-glowing coals for about 5 minutes. Cut into 2-inch-wide pieces. Makes about 10 servings.

Foil-wrapped Bread

Open or covered grill • Cooking time: 10–12 minutes

Not only French bread but rye, nut, and fruit breads can be warmed on the grill if wrapped in foil.

    ½ cup (¼ lb.) melted butter or margarine
    1 loaf bread (1 lb.), split lengthwise or
      sliced

Brush melted butter over bread halves or on one side of each slice. Reassemble loaf and wrap tightly in a double sheet of heavy-duty foil. Place on grill 4 to 6 inches above a solid bed of low-glowing coals for 10 to 12 minutes. If needed, cut into slices to serve. Makes about 10 servings.

Baked Breads from the Barbecue

Covered grill • Cooking time: 50–60 minutes

Freshly baked bread, right from the grill? Why not? It can cook alongside meat on a covered barbecue. You'll need a mercury-type oven thermometer, positioned on the edge of the grill, to be sure you maintain a constant temperature of about 350°. The grill should be 4 to 6 inches above a solid bed of low-glowing coals. Place bread on the coolest part of the grill—not directly over hot coals—and check the temperature every 15 minutes. Move the pan often so the bread cooks evenly.

Olive Pizza Bread

Combine 1 can (2¼ oz.) **sliced olives** (drained), 2 tablespoons melted **butter** or margarine, 2 teaspoons **instant minced onion,** 1 teaspoon

Worcestershire, dash of liquid **hot pepper seasoning,** and 1 cup shredded **Cheddar cheese;** set aside.

Stir together 1¼ cups **biscuit mix** (buttermilk baking mix) and ⅓ cup **milk** just until moistened. Pat dough evenly into a greased 9-inch round or square baking pan. Spoon olive mixture evenly over top; then sprinkle with 1 teaspoon **caraway seed.** Bake in covered barbecue at about 350° for about 50 minutes or until nicely browned on top and around edges. Turn out of pan and cut into wedges or wide slices. Makes 6 to 8 servings.

Parmesan Onion Bread

Stir together 2 cups all-purpose **flour** (unsifted), 2 teaspoons **baking powder,** ½ teaspoon **salt,** and ¾ cup grated **Parmesan cheese.** Cut in ¼ cup **butter** or margarine until mixture resembles coarse crumbs; set aside. In 1 tablespoon melted **butter** or margarine, cook 1 cup thinly sliced **green onion** and 2 cloves **garlic** (minced or pressed) until soft. Stir into flour mixture, adding 1 tablespoon **celery seed** or caraway seed, or toasted sesame seed. Lightly beat 1 **egg** with ¾ cup **milk** and stir into flour mixture until blended. Spread dough into a greased 9-inch round or square baking pan.

Bake in covered barbecue at 350° for about 1 hour or until bread is crusty and browned and begins to pull away from sides of pan. Turn out of pan onto rack and let stand until cool enough to cut into wide slices with a serrated knife. Makes 6 to 8 servings.

Baked Onion Loaf Bread

Covered grill • Cooking time: About 45 minutes

Here's an easy baked bread. It's made from hot roll mix and cooks in less than an hour in a covered barbecue.

    1 package (about 14 oz.) hot roll mix
      Warm water
    3 tablespoons instant toasted onion
    ¼ teaspoon *each* celery seed and thyme
      leaves
      Butter or margarine

Prepare hot roll mix as directed on package, except increase to 1 cup the warm water in which you dissolve the yeast. To the dough, add toasted onion, celery seed, and thyme; mix well. Cover and let rise in a warm place until doubled (about 45 minutes).

Punch dough down and spoon into a well-greased 9 by 5-inch loaf pan. Cover and let rise in a warm place until doubled (about 30 minutes). Bake in a covered barbecue at about 375° (see instructions for Baked Breads from the Barbecue, page 87) for about 45 minutes or until well browned all over. Turn loaf out of pan and keep warm. Serve with butter. Makes 1 loaf.

Hot Herb Bread

Open or covered grill • Cooking time: About 10 minutes

Brush the herb-butter mixture on presliced bread, then wrap in foil and heat.

    1 cup (½ lb.) butter or margarine, at room
        temperature
    ¾ cup minced chives (fresh, frozen, or
        freeze-dried)
    ¾ cup lightly packed minced parsley
    1 tablespoon dry basil
    2 loaves (1 lb. *each*) French bread, split
        lengthwise

Cream butter with chives, parsley, and basil. Spread on bread halves and reassemble loaves. Wrap each tightly in heavy-duty foil and place on grill 4 to 6 inches above a solid bed of low-glowing coals for about 10 minutes. Cut into 2-inch-wide slices. Makes about 20 servings.

Dutch-oven Peas in Pods

Open or covered grill • Cooking time: About 15 minutes

Here's a fun way of serving tender young peas that we think will go over well at your next barbecue. Let everyone shell his or her own peas. We found it's easiest to just put the whole pod between your teeth, bite lightly, and pull—the peas pop into your mouth. *(Pictured on page 63)*

    2 pounds whole, unshelled peas
    2 tablespoons water

Rinse peas well (but do not dry) and place in a cast-iron Dutch oven or frying pan; add water. Cover with pan lid or heavy-duty foil and place on grill 4 to 6 inches above a solid bed of medium-glowing coals. Cook, stirring every 5 minutes, for about 15 minutes or until peas are tender to bite. Makes 4 servings.

Grilled Potato Slices

Open or covered grill • Cooking time: About 30 minutes

Cut unpeeled potatoes lengthwise in ¼-inch-thick slices and brush with butter and garlic salt before cooking them directly on the grill.

    4 to 6 large russet potatoes
        Melted butter or margarine
        Garlic salt

Scrub potatoes well but do not peel. Cut lengthwise into ¼-inch-thick slices and generously brush both sides with butter. Sprinkle lightly with garlic salt.

Place on grill 4 to 6 inches above a solid bed of medium-glowing coals. Cook, turning as needed to brown both sides, for about 30 minutes or until potatoes are soft when pierced. Makes 4 to 6 servings.

Stuffed Potatoes

Open or covered grill • Cooking time: About 1¼ hours

Baked potatoes are mashed in their skins and seasoned with bacon bits, green onion, and shredded cheese. *(Pictured on page 31)*

    4 medium-size russet potatoes
    ½ cup (¼ lb.) butter or margarine
    4 green onions, thinly sliced (including
        tops)
    8 strips bacon, crisply fried and crumbled
    1½ cups shredded Cheddar cheese

Wash and scrub potatoes thoroughly. Prick skin in several places with a fork; wrap each tightly in heavy-duty foil. Place on grill 4 to 6 inches above a solid bed of medium-glowing coals and cook, shifting packet several times, for about 1 hour or until potatoes are soft when squeezed.

Split cooked potatoes lengthwise. With a fork, slightly mash potato and mix 1 tablespoon butter into each half. Evenly spoon onion, bacon, and cheese over each, mixing lightly. Serve immediately. Or just before serving, broil 4 to 6 inches below heat until cheese is bubbly. Makes 8 servings.

Foil-wrapped Vegetables from the Grill

Open or covered grill • Cooking time: 15–60 minutes

Foil-wrapping is the simplest way to prepare vegetables for the barbecue. Our suggestions for seasonings and garnishes are pictured on page 47, but you may want to try other combinations or just season with salt and pepper or a little butter.

Wash vegetables thoroughly but do not pat dry —excess water helps to create enough moisture to steam-cook most vegetables. Wrap tightly in heavy-duty foil, then place on grill directly over coals (for a divided fire bed this means near the edges of the cooking grill).

Each of the following recipes yields approximately four servings:

Artichokes

Snip off top third from 4 **artichokes,** also snip off tips of remaining leaves. Wash thoroughly, pulling leaves apart slightly as you wash. Place on individual sheets of heavy-duty foil. Into center of each artichoke, pour ½ teaspoon **olive oil** or salad oil. Sprinkle tops with 1 tablespoon thinly sliced mild **onion** and **salt** and **pepper** to taste. Wrap tightly and place on grill 4 to 6 inches above a solid bed of medium-glowing coals. Cook, shifting individual packets occasionally, for 55 to 60 minutes or until bottom of artichoke is tender when pierced. Garnish with **lemon wedges.**

Asparagus

Break off fibrous ends from 1½ to 2 pounds **asparagus.** Wash asparagus well; place on heavy-duty foil. Season with **salt** and **pepper** to taste and dot with about 2 tablespoons **butter** or margarine. Close tightly and place on grill 4 to 6 inches above a solid bed of medium-glowing coals. Cook, shifting packet occasionally, for 15 to 20 minutes or until done to your liking when pierced. Five minutes before serving, sauté 3 tablespoons **pine nuts** or slivered almonds in 1 tablespoon **butter** or margarine over medium-high heat just until browned (about 3 minutes). Sprinkle over cooked asparagus.

Carrots

Peel 1 pound medium-size **carrots** (cut into 1-inch lengths, if desired). Place on heavy-duty foil. Season with **salt** and **pepper** to taste and dot with 2 tablespoons **butter** or margarine. Top with 1 tablespoon grated **lemon peel.** Wrap tightly and place on grill 4 to 6 inches above a solid bed of medium-glowing coals. Cook, shifting packet occasionally, for 25 to 30 minutes (about 15 minutes for sliced carrots) or until done to your liking.

Green Beans

Break off tips and remove strings from 1 pound **green beans.** Wash and place on heavy-duty foil. Season with **salt** and **pepper** to taste and 1 teaspoon **savory leaves;** dot with 2 tablespoons **butter** or margarine. Wrap tightly and place on grill 4 to 6 inches above a solid bed of medium-glowing coals. Cook, shifting packet occasionally, for about 20 minutes or until done to your liking when pierced. Just before serving, sprinkle 2 tablespoons toasted sliced **almonds** over cooked beans.

New Potatoes

Wash 1 pound small **new potatoes** thoroughly. Peel a 1-inch-wide piece of skin off each potato all the way around its circumference. Place potatoes together on heavy-duty foil. Season with **salt** and **pepper** to taste and 2 teaspoons finely chopped **parsley;** dot with 2 tablespoons **butter** or margarine. Wrap tightly and place on grill 4 to 6 inches above a solid bed of medium-glowing coals. Cook, shifting packet occasionally, for 50 to 55 minutes or until tender when pierced.

Peas

Shell 2 pounds of **peas** and rinse thoroughly. Place on heavy-duty foil. Scatter ¼ cup thinly sliced **mushrooms** over top. Season to taste with **salt** and **pepper** and dot with 2 tablespoons **butter** or margarine. Wrap tightly and place on grill 4 to 6 inches above a solid bed of medium-glowing coals. Cook, shifting packet occasionally, for about 20 minutes or until tender to bite.

Squash

Peel and cut about 1½ pounds **winter squash** (such as banana or hubbard) into spears (about 1 inch wide and 6 inches long). Scrape away any seeds and fibrous material; rinse thoroughly. Place on heavy-duty foil. Season with **salt** and **pepper** to taste and dot with 3 tablespoons **butter** or margarine. Sprinkle 2 tablespoons lightly packed **brown sugar** over spears. Wrap tightly and place on grill 4 to 6 inches above a solid bed of medium-glowing coals. Cook, shifting packet occasionally, for 25 to 30 minutes or until done to your liking.

(Continued on next page)

Zucchini-Tomato Casserole

Wash 2 medium-size **zucchini** and cut into ½-inch slices. Wash and peel 2 medium-size **tomatoes** and cut into small wedges. Thinly slice 1 medium-size **onion.** On heavy-duty foil, arrange zucchini, tomatoes, and onion wedges in 2 layers, using half of each vegetable per layer. Sprinkle *each* layer with **salt** and **pepper** to taste and ¼ teaspoon **oregano leaves.** Pour 1 tablespoon **olive oil** or salad oil over top. Seal tightly and place on grill 4 to 6 inches above a solid bed of medium-glowing coals. Cook, shifting packet occasionally, for 25 to 30 minutes or until done to your liking when pierced.

Vegetable Kebabs

Open or covered grill • Cooking time: 10–15 minutes

Skewered vegetables simplify the problem of a side dish for barbecued meats because they cook right alongside them on the grill. *(Pictured on page 31)*

    4 medium-size zucchini, cut in 1-inch
        lengths
    2 medium-size mild onions, cut in wedges
    12 to 16 large mushrooms
        Melted butter

Onto 4 sturdy metal skewers, alternately thread zucchini, onion, and mushrooms. Place on lightly greased grill 4 to 6 inches above a solid bed of low-glowing coals. Cook, turning often and basting with melted butter or other basting sauce, for 10 to 15 minutes or until done to your liking. Makes 4 servings.

Corn on the Cob

Open or covered grill • Cooking time: 12–20 minutes

Many barbecue enthusiasts have their own way to grill corn on the cob. Some add flavored butters or herbs, some use unhusked ears. Here are a few of the variations:

• Pull husks back, remove silk, replace husks, and soak in ice water for about 30 minutes. Drain well and place on grill 4 to 6 inches above a solid bed of glowing coals for 15 to 20 minutes, turning occasionally.

• Pull husks back and remove silk. Replace husks and wire them into place (with any fine wire) at center and near tip of cob, covering kernels as well as possible. Place on grill 4 to 6 inches above a solid bed of glowing coals for 15 to 20 minutes, turning occasionally. Snip wires with wire cutter (be sure to wear gloves).

• Husk and remove silk from 6 ears of corn. Place ears on individual sheets of heavy-duty foil. Combine ¼ cup melted butter or margarine and 1½ tablespoons soy sauce; pour about 1 tablespoon of the mixture over each ear. Wrap tightly and place on grill 4 to 6 inches above a solid bed of glowing coals for 12 to 15 minutes, turning occasionally.

• Pull husks back, remove silk, brush corn generously with butter or margarine. Replace husks and place ears on grill 4 to 6 inches above a solid bed of medium-glowing coals. Dip a clean piece of burlap in warm water, wring it out slightly, and place it over ears so they will steam. Grill ears for 10 minutes on one side, then remove burlap and turn ears. Sprinkle burlap with more water and re-cover corn. Grill for 10 minutes longer.

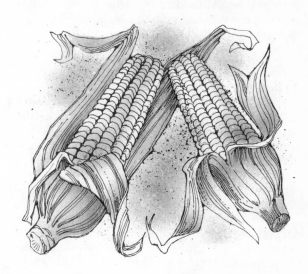

Tomatoes Provençal

Open grill • Cooking time: About 10 minutes

Wedges of ripe, tangy tomatoes merely warm in this buttery sauce assembled on the barbecue grill. *(Pictured on page 71)*

    4 tablespoons butter or margarine
    2 tablespoons *each* finely chopped green
        onion or shallots and parsley
    ½ teaspoon sugar
    3 tablespoons dry white wine or dry
        vermouth
    3 medium-size tomatoes, peeled,
        quartered, and seeded
    2 cloves garlic, minced or pressed
        Salt and pepper

In a heavy frying pan or metal dish, melt 2 tablespoons of the butter over hottest coals. Add onion, parsley, sugar, and wine. Bring mixture to a boil, stirring occasionally. Add tomatoes to pan and mix gently until heated through. Add the remaining 2 tablespoons butter and garlic; stir until butter melts. Remove from heat at once, season with salt and pepper, and serve. Makes 4 to 6 servings.

Foil-wrapped Fruit

Open or covered grill • Cooking time: 5–12 minutes

Foil-wrapped fruit can accompany grilled meats, poultry, or fish; or it can serve as dessert to conclude a barbecue dinner. You just heat it for a short time on the grill. The following recipes yield approximately 4 servings.

Apples

Wash, peel (if desired), and slice 4 medium-size **apples** and place on a sheet of heavy-duty foil. Sprinkle with 2 teaspoons **lemon juice.** Dot with 2 tablespoons **butter** or margarine; sprinkle with 1 tablespoon **sugar,** and ground **cinnamon** or coriander to taste. Wrap tightly and place on grill 4 to 6 inches above a solid bed of glowing or medium-glowing coals. Cook, shifting packet often, for 12 to 15 minutes or until done to your liking and heated through. Serve with barbecued pork or as dessert with a dollop of sweetened whipped cream or sour cream.

Bananas

Peel and slice or quarter 4 medium-size **bananas** and place on heavy-duty foil. Dot with 1 tablespoon **butter** or margarine and 1 teaspoon *each* **sugar** and ground **cinnamon.** (Or use unpeeled bananas and make a slit about 3 inches long in the skin. Drizzle about 1 tablespoon **honey** into each opening and let stand ½ hour. Place on individual sheets of heavy-duty foil.) Wrap tightly and place on grill 4 to 6 inches above a solid bed of glowing or medium-glowing coals. Cook, shifting packet (or packets) often, for 5 to 8 minutes (if using whole bananas, for 8 to 10 minutes) or until heated through. Serve as dessert.

Grapefruit

Cut 2 large **grapefruit** in half, remove seeds, and loosen sections from skin and section membranes. Place, cut-side-up, on individual sheets of heavy-duty foil. Dot each top with 1 teaspoon **butter** or margarine; pour 1 tablespoon **rum** or dry sherry over each half. Wrap tightly and place on grill, cut-side-up, 4 to 6 inches above a solid bed of glowing coals. Cook, shifting individual packets occasionally, for 8 to 10 minutes or until heated through. Serve as dessert or as first course for a brunch.

Oranges

Peel 3 or 4 large seedless **oranges,** divide into segments, and place on heavy-duty foil. Dot with 1 tablespoon **butter** or margarine and 1 teaspoon *each* **sugar** and ground **cinnamon** or dry rosemary. Seal tightly and place on grill 4 to 6 inches above a solid bed of glowing or medium-glowing coals. Cook, shifting packet occasionally, for 6 to 8 minutes or until heated through. Serve with poultry, beef, or fish.

Peaches

Peel 4 medium-size **peaches** and remove pits; slice peaches and place on heavy-duty foil. Sprinkle with 2 teaspoons **lemon juice,** dot with 1 tablespoon **butter** or margarine, and sprinkle on 2 tablespoons lightly packed **brown sugar.** Seal tightly and place on grill 4 to 6 inches above a solid bed of glowing or medium-glowing coals. Cook, shifting packet often, for 6 to 8 minutes or until heated through. Serve over ice cream or pound cake for dessert or as an accompaniment to ham or poultry.

Pears

Peel, core, and slice 4 large **pears;** place on heavy-duty foil. Sprinkle with 2 teaspoons **lemon juice,** dot with 1 tablespoon **butter** or margarine, and sprinkle on 1 teaspoon *each* **sugar** and ground **ginger** (or ½ teaspoon slivered candied ginger). (Or peel and core pears but leave whole. Into each opening, put 1 teaspoon **butter** or margarine, ½ teaspoon *each* **sugar** and ground **ginger.** Place on individual sheets of heavy-duty foil.) Wrap tightly and place on grill 4 to 6 inches above a solid bed of glowing or medium-glowing coals. Cook, shifting packet (or packets) occasionally, for 5 to 7 minutes (if using whole pears, for 10 to 12 minutes) or until heated through. Serve as dessert with a dollop of sweetened whipped cream or sour cream.

Pineapple

Peel and core a fresh **pineapple** and cut it into 8 lengthwise spears. Place on heavy-duty foil. Drizzle 3 or 4 tablespoons **honey** on spears and wrap tightly. Place on grill 4 to 6 inches above a solid bed of glowing or medium-glowing coals. Cook, shifting packet occasionally, for 8 to 10 minutes or until heated through. Serve with ham or other barbecued pork or as a first course for brunch.

Desserts

Bring an outdoor meal to a sweet conclusion —not with ready-made desserts or ones that take advance preparation, but with these tempting examples, all prepared on the barbecue. They're designed either to cook while you're eating or simply to warm over the coals at the last minute.

Rum Babas with Peaches

Open or covered grill • Cooking time: 15–20 minutes

Canned rum baba cakes are the base for this quick dessert. Fresh peaches or nectarines go on top, and flaming rum, ignited at the barbecue table, can be the finishing touch.

- 1 can (12 oz.) rum baba cakes (4 cakes)
- 2 large peaches or nectarines, peeled and halved
- 3 tablespoons rum (optional)

Arrange rum baba cakes in a greased shallow foil pan or flameproof dish; pour over syrup from the can. Place a peach half, cut-side-down, on top of each cake. Cover pan with a sheet of heavy-duty foil.

Bank about 10 low-glowing coals on each side of fire grill and place cooking grill 4 to 6 inches above coals. Place babas in center of grill so that no part of pan is directly over coals. Cook for about 15 minutes or until cakes and fruit are heated throughout.

Heat rum in a small flameproof container directly over coals. Ignite and carefully pour over peaches. Makes 4 servings.

Chocolate Sundae Pudding

Covered grill • Cooking time: About 45 minutes

This rich layered dessert can bake in a covered barbecue while you're eating. A crusty topping forms over chocolate pudding with a fudge sauce layer below. Serve it hot with whipped cream or ice cream.

- 1 cup all-purpose flour
- 2 teaspoons baking powder
- ½ teaspoon salt
- 2 tablespoons unsweetened cocoa
- ⅔ cup sugar
- ½ cup *each* milk and chopped walnuts
- 2 tablespoons melted butter or margarine
- 1 teaspoon vanilla
  Chocolate topping (recipe follows)
- 1 cup boiling water
  Whipped cream or ice cream (optional)

Combine flour, baking powder, salt, cocoa, and sugar. Sift into a mixing bowl. Add milk, nuts, butter, and vanilla; blend well. Pour into a well-greased, 9-inch square metal pan or flameproof baking dish.

Prepare Chocolate topping and spread evenly over batter. Slowly pour boiling water over all—do not stir.

Bank 20 low-glowing coals on each side of fire grill. (If low-glowing coals remain from first barbecue fire, add 5 or 6 briquets to each side to maintain a constant temperature.) Place cooking grill 4 to 6 inches above coals. Place baking pan in center of grill so that no part is directly over coals. Cover barbecue and

adjust dampers according to manufacturer's directions.

Cook for about 45 minutes and then test for doneness. Pudding should be slightly crusty on top and firm. Continue checking every 5 minutes until desired doneness is reached. Spoon into individual dishes and top with whipped cream or ice cream, if desired. Makes 6 servings.

Chocolate topping. Combine ¼ cup granulated **sugar,** ½ cup **brown sugar,** 3 tablespoons unsweetened **cocoa,** ½ teaspoon **salt,** and 1 teaspoon **vanilla.**

Dessert Fondue Sauces

Open grill • Cooking time: ½–5 minutes

Rich dessert fondue is a delicious finale for informal meals, especially barbecues where enough low-glowing coals remain to keep the sauce warm. Simply prepare sauce ahead of time, then place it on the grill to heat and serve with fondue forks and a tray of bite-size bits of fruit, cake, or cookies for dipping.

Any flameproof dish or double-boiler about the size of a cereal bowl or larger will do. Just remember to keep an eye on the fondue at first—move it to a cooler part of the grill if you see any signs of boiling or scorching.

For dipping, allow approximately ½ to 1 cup of fruit plus 4 to 6 bite-size cubes of cake for each serving. You can use pieces of well-ripened peaches, pineapple, bananas, mangoes, and papayas, or whole seedless grapes, strawberries, raspberries, and pitted prunes. Try delicate cookies, angel food or pound cake, ladyfingers, and other small sweets. Each of the following recipes yields about 1 cup of sauce—enough for 4 to 6 servings.

Orange-Honey Fondue
In a small bowl, mix together ¼ cup **butter** or margarine (at room temperature), ½ cup **whipping cream,** and 2 tablespoons *each* **sugar, honey,** and **orange marmalade.** Pour into a flameproof dish and place on grill directly over coals. Bring to a full, vigorously foaming boil, stirring constantly. Cook for 30 seconds and then move to a cooler part of the grill to keep warm. Stir in 2 tablespoons **orange-flavored liqueur,** if desired. Serve with fruit (suggestions precede) and/or pieces of cake or small cookies.

Swiss Chocolate Fondue
For variety, try some of the flavored chocolates—coffee, almond, or hazelnut, for example—in place of milk chocolate. A dash of brandy, rum, crème de menthe, or coffee-flavored liqueur adds interest to the basic chocolate mixture.

Place 12 ounces **milk chocolate,** semisweet baking chocolate, or other flavored chocolate, and ¾ cup **whipping cream** in the top of a double-boiler; set over hot, not boiling, water to melt. Stir until well blended, then stir in 3 tablespoons **orange-flavored liqueur** or other liqueur. Pour into a flameproof dish (if necessary) and place on grill to keep warm (be careful not to overheat chocolate or it may scorch).

Toasted Pound Cake

Open grill • Cooking time: About 4 minutes

Slices of fresh or frozen pound cake toast quickly to a golden brown over low-glowing coals. Spoon sliced fruit, either cold or warmed (see Foil-wrapped Fruit, page 91) over top with a dollop of whipped or sour cream. A hinged wire broiler makes it easy to turn slices, otherwise you'll need a long-handled spatula.

> 1 fresh or frozen pound cake (10¾ oz.), cut in 1-inch-thick slices
> 2 cups sliced fruit
> Whipped or sour cream (optional)

Place pound cake slices in a hinged wire broiler; or, place slices on lightly greased grill 4 to 6 inches above a solid bed of low-glowing coals. Toast, turning often, just until brown (about 1 or 2 minutes on each side). Serve with sliced fruit and a dollop of whipped cream, if desired. Makes 6 to 8 servings.

Index

A Handy Metric Conversion Table

To change	To	Multiply by
ounces (oz.)	grams (g)	28
pounds (lbs.)	kilograms (kg)	0.45
teaspoons	milliliters (ml)	5
tablespoons	milliliters (ml)	15
fluid ounces (fl. oz.)	milliliters (ml)	30
cups	liters (l)	0.24
pints (pt.)	liters (l)	0.47
quarts (qt.)	liters (l)	0.95
gallons (gal.)	liters (l)	3.8
inches	centimeters (cm)	2.5
Fahrenheit temperature (°F)	*Celsius temperature (°C)*	*5/9 after subtracting 32*